Malaysian
Home
Cooking

Lee Sook Ching

 **Marshall Cavendish** Cuisine

To my parents, who brought me up
in the belief that a good life is a
combination of family and friends enjoying
a home-cooked meal in the relaxed
atmosphere of a happy home.

Contents

Meat

Soups

Vegetables

Noodles

Desserts and Snacks

Miscellaneous Favourites

Cooking Tips • 159

Glossary • 165

Weights & Measures • 175

I feel very happy that many people find
my recipes very easy to follow and that the recipes
turn out right, to the extent that they refer to
my cookbook as their cooking Bible.

Preface

Cooking styles have changed greatly since the 1970s. People are now more health-conscious. Obesity, diabetes, heart conditions and many other health problems are very common and people now realise that we are in control of our health, and we are what we eat. No longer do we insist that vegetables only taste good if they are fried in large quantities of cooking oil and a good spoonful of food enhancer. Today's cry is for 'less oil, less salt and no food enhancer'. Will the food be bland and unpalatable then? Definitely not! Onions, garlic, ginger, besides all the different spices available, can be used to give flavour to food. Instead of food enhancers, use stocks, which can be easily prepared from vegetables and stored in the freezer in one- or two-cup packs, ready for use when needed.

Most of the recipes in this book have been revised to suit the lifestyles and taste buds of today. The recipes are simple and easy-to-follow, and anybody can use them to produce delicious meals with confidence. And for those who prefer to eat brown unpolished rice, simply use it in place of white rice in the recipes. You may also substitute white meat for red meat if you do not take red meat. Be brave and dare to experiment. Cooking will then become interesting and fun!

To all my family and friends, my sincere thanks for all the help given in so many ways, and for becoming my guinea pigs so willingly. It is my belief that a happy family is one that sits together in the relaxed atmosphere of a home, enjoying one another's company over a tasty home-cooked meal. A group of friends can also do the same.

I hope you will enjoy using these recipes and cooking for your family and friends.

Lee Sook Ching

Rice

Chicken Rice in Clay Pot

Preparation time 15–20 min • *Cooking time* 30 min • *Serves* 4–6

Chicken ½ (about 900 g)
Dried Chinese mushrooms 5
Ginger 1-cm knob
Salt 1 tsp
Light soy sauce 2 tsp
Dark soy sauce 1½ tsp
Cooking oil 3 Tbsp
Shallots 4, sliced
Rice 450 g
Chinese sausages 1 pair
Spring onions 2, chopped

1. Clean and cut chicken into small pieces. Soak mushrooms till soft, then wash and cut into halves or quarters. Pound ginger and squeeze for juice. Season chicken pieces with ginger juice, ½ tsp salt, light and dark soy sauce.

2. Heat cooking oil and brown shallots. Add chicken and mushrooms and fry till chicken pieces are firm.

3. Wash rice, add the remaining salt and enough water, and put it to boil in a clay pot. When rice is cooked and almost dry, add fried ingredients together with the whole sausages, placing the sausages on top. Cover and allow rice to finish cooking on very low heat. Alternatively, use a rice cooker instead of a clay pot.

4. When rice is cooked, remove sausages and slice diagonally into 1-cm sections. Return sliced sausages to rice and stir to mix all ingredients thoroughly. Season to taste and serve rice garnished with spring onions.

Note: Clay pot should be soaked in a basin of water for an hour or so before use to prevent it from cracking.

Chicken Rice, Hainanese Style

Preparation time 30 min • *Cooking time* 1 hr • *Serves* 6–8

Chicken 1 (1.5–2 kg)
Sesame oil 2 tsp
Light soy sauce 1 tsp
Rice 450 g
Cooking oil 2 Tbsp
Garlic 4 cloves, finely chopped
Chicken stock cube 1
Salt 2 tsp
Sugar 2 tsp

1. In a large pan, boil enough water to cover the chicken. When boiling, put in chicken, turn heat to low and cook covered for 10 minutes. Turn off heat and leave chicken to cook in the water for another 40 minutes. Remove chicken and put into a basin of cold water for 15 minutes. Hang chicken up to dry, then brush with 1 tsp sesame oil mixed with soy sauce. Cut off legs, wing tips and neck. Put them back to boil in stock.

2. Wash rice and drain. Heat 1 Tbsp oil and brown garlic. Add rice, stir-fry for 1 minute, then add enough stock to cook it. Add stock cube and 1 tsp each of salt, sugar and the remaining sesame oil and cook until liquid is absorbed and rice is cooked.

3. Cut chicken into 2.5-cm wide pieces. Serve with the rice, *chilli sauce and stock as soup.

*Chilli Sauce

Red chillies 10
Garlic 1 clove
Ginger 5-cm knob, ground
Cooking oil 1 Tbsp
Salt 1 tsp
Sugar 1 tsp
Tomato ketchup 1 Tbsp
Vinegar 1 Tbsp
Sesame oil 1 tsp
Chicken stock 4 Tbsp

1. Pound together chillies, garlic and ginger until very fine. Heat 1 Tbsp oil and fry pounded ingredients. Add salt, sugar, tomato ketchup, vinegar, sesame oil and chicken stock. When boiled, season the sauce and cool.

Chicken Rice, Hainanese Style

Savoury Rice

Preparation time 15–20 min • *Cooking time* 30 min • *Serves* 4–6

Fillet steak 300 g
Ginger juice extracted from
   2.5-cm knob ginger
Tapioca flour 2 tsp
Light soy sauce 2 tsp
Dark soy sauce 1 tsp
Cooking oil 2 Tbsp
A shake of pepper
Shallots 6–8, sliced
Rice 450 g
Salt 1 tsp
Spring onions 2, chopped

1. Slice steak thinly, cutting across the grain. Marinate in a mixture of ginger juice, tapioca flour, light and dark soy sauce, 1 Tbsp cooking oil and pepper.

2. Heat remaining oil in a frying pan and brown the shallots. Keep browned shallots for garnishing. Add seasoned steak to hot oil and stir-fry for 1 minute. Remove the pan from heat.

3. Wash rice and boil it with salt added to enough water. When rice is almost cooked and water is all absorbed, add in the lightly cooked steak. Cover pan tightly and allow rice to finish cooking on very low heat.

4. When rice is well cooked, loosen the grains with chopsticks or a fork and at the same time mix the meat with the rice. Season rice to taste and serve it garnished with browned shallots and spring onions.

Fried Rice

Preparation time 10 min • *Cooking time* 10 min • *Serves* 4–6

Prawns ½ cup
BBQ pork (*char siew*) ½ cup
Chinese sausages 1 pair
Eggs 2
Salt ¾ tsp
A shake of pepper
Cooking oil 1½ Tbsp
Shallots 4, sliced
Green peas ½ cup
Light soy sauce 2 tsp
Cooked rice 3 cups
Spring onions 2, chopped

1. Shell and devein prawns. Dice prawns, BBQ pork and Chinese sausages. Beat eggs with ¼ tsp salt and a shake of pepper.

2. Heat ½ Tbsp cooking oil and scramble eggs till set. Remove. Heat the remaining oil, brown shallots, then fry prawns, sausages and BBQ pork together for 1 minute. Add green peas, the remaining salt and soy sauce and stir-fry for another minute.

3. Add loosened cooked rice and stir-fry all together for 5 minutes. Mix in scrambled egg. Season to taste and serve garnished with chopped spring onions.

Rice with Long Beans

Preparation time 20 min • *Cooking time* 30 min • *Serves* 4–6

Cooking oil 1 Tbsp
Shallots 6–8, sliced
Pork or chicken 250 g, minced
Dried prawns 2 Tbsp, chopped coarsely
Salt 2 tsp
Light soy sauce 1 tsp
Water 2–3 Tbsp
Long beans 10–12, diced
Rice 300 g
A shake of pepper

1. Heat cooking oil and brown the shallots. Set aside for garnishing. In the same oil, stir-fry minced pork or chicken and dried prawns. Add $1/2$ tsp salt and soy sauce with 2–3 Tbsp water. Cook for 5 minutes. Add long beans. Mix it thoroughly with meat. Remove all ingredients and set aside.

2. Wash rice and boil with enough water and the remaining salt. When rice is dry and almost cooked, add cooked ingredients and allow rice to finish cooking over very low heat.

3. When rice is cooked, stir well to mix the ingredients. Season to taste and serve garnished with browned shallots and *sambal belacan* (page 123) if desired.

Dried Prawns (*Udang kering* or *Har mai*)

These are sun-dried salted, steamed prawns. Soak them in water for about 20 minutes to remove excess salt before using. Dried prawns may be ground, chopped coarsely or left whole and fried to flavour dishes.

Salt Fish Rice

Preparation time 15–20 min • *Cooking time* 30 min • *Serves* 4–6

Cooking oil 1 Tbsp
Shallots 6
Salt fish 100 g, diced
Pork or chicken meat 250 g, minced
Dried prawns 2 Tbsp, soaked and
    chopped coarsely
Rice 300 g
Salt 1 tsp
A shake of pepper
Spring onion 2–3 tsp, chopped

1. Heat cooking oil and brown shallots. Set aside for garnishing. In the same oil, fry salt fish till slightly brown. Remove. Fry minced meat and dried prawns till well cooked. Remove and mix with salt fish.

2. Wash and boil rice with enough water and $1/2$ tsp salt. When rice is almost dry, add salt fish and meat mixture and allow rice to finish cooking on very low heat.

3. When rice is cooked, stir to mix all ingredients thoroughly. Season to taste with remaining salt and pepper and serve garnished with spring onion and browned shallots.

Note: Instead of pork or chicken, flaked steamed or fried fish meat can also be used. Any kind of salt fish (with few bones) can also be used. Long beans, cut into 0.5-cm sections may be added, if desired. This dish may be served with *sambal belacan* (page 123).

Savoury Glutinous Rice

Preparation time 25 min • Cooking time 1 hr • Serves 6–8

Glutinous rice 500 g, soaked overnight
Fresh prawns 250 g
Dried prawns 2 Tbsp, soaked
Dried oysters 100 g, soaked
Dried Chinese mushrooms 4, soaked
Cooking oil 2 Tbsp
Shallots 10–12, sliced
Light soy sauce 2 Tbsp
Oyster sauce 1 Tbsp
Sesame oil 1 tsp
Salt $1/_2$ tsp
Water $1/_2$ cup
Spring onions 2, chopped

1. Rinse rice and drain well.

2. Shell and devein fresh prawns. Dice fresh prawns, dried prawns, dried oysters and mushrooms.

3. Heat cooking oil and brown shallots. Set aside. In the same oil, fry fresh prawns, dried prawns, dried oysters and mushrooms for 2 minutes. Add rice and toss to mix thoroughly.

4. Mix together soy sauce, oyster sauce, sesame oil, salt and water and add this mixture gradually to the fried ingredients. Stir to mix, cover and cook on very low heat till rice is cooked. Turn rice and stir every 10 minutes to prevent burning.

5. Garnish with spring onions and browned shallots to serve.

Loh Mai Kai
(Chicken in Glutinous Rice)

Preparation time 20–25 min • Cooking time 50–60 min • Serves 10

Glutinous rice 500 g, soaked overnight
Chicken $1/_2$
Light soy sauce 2 Tbsp
Oyster sauce 2 Tbsp
Sesame oil 2 tsp
Sugar 3 tsp
BBQ pork (*char siew*) 100 g
Pork 225 g
Dark soy sauce $1/_2$ tsp
Pepper $1/_4$ tsp
Dried Chinese mushrooms 5, soaked to soften and halved
Water $1/_4$ cup
Cornflour 1 Tbsp, mixed with $1/_4$ cup water
Cooking oil 3 Tbsp
Salt $1/_2$ tsp
Coriander leaves 2–3 tsp, chopped

1. Rinse rice and drain. Cut chicken into 1-cm pieces. Season with $1/_2$ Tbsp light soy sauce, 1 Tbsp oyster sauce, 1 tsp sesame oil and 1 tsp sugar.

2. Slice BBQ pork into 10 pieces. Dice pork into 1-cm cubes. Season with $1/_2$ Tbsp light soy sauce, dark soy sauce, remaining oyster sauce and sesame oil, $1^1/_2$ tsp sugar and pepper.

3. Heat 1 Tbsp cooking oil and fry chicken until cooked and all the gravy is absorbed. Remove and set aside.

4. Heat another 1 Tbsp cooking oil, add pork and toss for 1 minute. Add mushrooms and water, cover and simmer for 10 minutes. Thicken gravy with cornflour mixture when pork is cooked. Set aside.

5. Mix drained rice with the remaining cooking oil, light soy sauce, sugar and the salt.

6. Divide chicken, BBQ pork, fried pork and mushrooms into 10 equal portions. Place into 10 bowls. Divide rice into 10 portions and cover the ingredients in each bowl with a portion of rice. Bowls should only be half full.

7. Steam over boiling water for about 30 minutes or till rice is well-cooked. Turn the bowls of rice onto serving dishes so that the meat is on top. Serve garnished with chopped coriander leaves.

Note: Wrap ingredients in lotus leaves and steam as Lotus Leaf Rice.

Lontong

(Rice in Banana Leaves)

Preparation time 10 min • *Cooking time* 2–3 hr • *Serves* 4

Rice 2 cups
Banana leaves or aluminium foil

1. Soften banana leaves by scalding them. Clean and dry them. Wash rice and drain.

2. Wrap rice in banana leaves loosely to get cylindrical packets about 15-cm long and about 2.5–5-cm wide. Fasten with toothpicks or staple together. Alternatively, wrap rice in aluminium foil. Remember that there must be room in the packets for the rice to expand while cooking. The packets should be no more than three quarters full. Place rice packets in a large pan filled with water and boil for 2–3 hours. If necessary, add more water to the pan.

3. Cool, slice into 1.5-cm sections and serve.

Note: *Lontong* is usually served with *Gado-Gado* (page 89), *Masak Lodeh* (page 91) or *Sambal Kelapa* (page 100).

Nasi Lemak

(Coconut Milk Rice)

Preparation time 10 min • *Cooking time* 30–40 min • *Serves* 6–8

Coconut 1, peeled and grated
Rice 500 g
Salt 1 tsp
Pandan (screwpine) leaves 2

1. Extract 3 cups coconut milk from grated coconut.

2. Wash rice and drain it. Put rice into a steamer, add salt, pandan leaves and coconut milk and steam over boiling water for 30 minutes. Stir rice after 30 minutes, then test to check if it is cooked. If not, steam for another 10 minutes or until cooked. Remove pandan leaves and loosen rice with a fork.

3. Serve with Beef Rendang (page 39), Fried Fish with Turmeric (page 59), Fried Tamarind Prawns (page 69), Sambal Ikan Bilis (page 74), hard-boiled eggs and cucumber.

Nasi Briyani

(Spiced Rice with Chicken)

Preparation time 30–35 min • *Cooking time* 1 hr • *Serves* 4–6

Chicken 1 (about 900 g)
Garlic 1 clove
Ginger 5-cm knob
Chillies 2
Poppy seeds 1 Tbsp
Cashew nuts 10
Almonds 10
Ghee 2 Tbsp
Cloves 5
Cinnamon stick 5-cm length
Shallots 1 cup, sliced
Salt 2 tsp
Curry powder 1 tsp
Yoghurt $^1/_2$ cup
Coconut $^1/_2$, grated
Rice 400 g, washed

1. Cut chicken into 4 pieces. Grind together garlic, ginger, chillies, poppy seeds, cashew nuts and almonds.

2. Heat ghee and fry cloves, cinnamon stick and shallots. Add chicken pieces, 1 tsp salt, ground ingredients and curry powder. Stir to mix and cook covered for 10 minutes. Add yoghurt and simmer till chicken is tender and mixture is thick.

3. Extract 1–2 cups coconut milk from grated coconut. Add coconut milk and the remaining salt to the rice and cook it. When the rice has absorbed all the milk, make a well in the centre and put in the chicken mixture. Cover and allow rice to finish cooking over very low heat.

4. Serve with a chutney or *acar*.

Nasi Biryani (Spiced Rice with Chicken)

Nasi Kunyit
(Yellow Rice)

Preparation time 20 min • *Cooking time* 40 min • *Serves* 6–8

Fresh turmeric (*kunyit*) 5–7-cm knob
Glutinous rice 500 g
Dried sour fruit (*asam gelugur*) 1 slice
Peppercorns 10–15
Pandan (screwpine) leaves 2
Coconut $^1/_2$, grated
Salt 1 tsp

1. Clean turmeric and pound till fine. Place it in a piece of muslin and tie it up firmly. Wash glutinous rice and soak it in water with the turmeric bag and dried sour fruit slices for at least 3 hours or overnight for best results. Rinse soaked rice under a running tap and drain it.

2. Put rice in a steamer with peppercorns and pandan leaves and steam over boiling water for 20–30 minutes. While rice is being steamed, extract $^1/_2$ cup thick coconut milk from grated coconut. Add salt to the coconut milk.

3. When rice is cooked, dish it into a large bowl and mix it with the thick coconut milk so that the rice grains are loosened. Return rice to the steamer and steam for another 10 minutes. When the rice is well cooked, it is soft, shiny and in loose grains. Serve with Chicken Curry (page 44), Beef Rendang (page 39) or Beef Curry (page 40).

Pork Broth

Preparation time 25 min • Cooking time 2 hr • Serves 4

Rice $^1/_2$ cup
Water about 6 cups
Pork 300 g, finely minced
Light soy sauce 2 tsp
Salt 1 tsp
A shake of pepper
Tapioca flour 2 tsp
Pig's liver (optional) 75 g
Sesame oil 1 tsp
Preserved cabbage (*tong choy*) 2 tsp
Spring onions 2, chopped

1. Wash rice and put it to boil with water. When it boils, turn down the heat and allow broth to simmer for 1–1$^1/_2$ hours.

2. Mix minced pork thoroughly with 1$^1/_2$ tsp soy sauce, $^1/_2$ tsp salt, pepper and tapioca flour. Shape meat into little balls 2.5-cm in diameter. Wash and cut liver into very thin slices. Season it with remaining salt and soy sauce, and pepper.

3. When broth is ready, add meatballs to it and cook for a further 3–4 minutes. When meat is cooked, add liver slices and as soon as broth boils again, turn off heat. Season broth and add sesame oil if desired. Serve it in a warmed dish and sprinkle preserved cabbage, spring onions and pepper on top.

Fish Broth

Preparation time 25 min • Cooking time 1$^1/_2$–1$^3/_4$ hr • Serves 4

Rice $^1/_2$ cup
Water 6 cups
Pomfret or threadfin fillet 300 g
Light soy sauce 2 tsp
Sesame oil (optional) 1 tsp
Cooking oil $^1/_2$ Tbsp
Salt $^1/_2$ tsp
A good shake of pepper
Ginger 6 slices, finely shredded
Preserved cabbage (*tong choy*) 2 tsp
Spring onions 2, chopped
Coriander leaves 1 sprig, chopped
A shake of pepper

1. Wash rice and boil with 6 cups water. When it boils, turn down the heat and allow the broth to simmer for 1–1$^1/_2$ hours.

2. Wash and slice fish thinly. Marinate the slices in a mixture of soy sauce, sesame oil (optional), cooking oil, salt and a good shake of pepper.

3. Place fish slices, ginger strips and preserved cabbage in a large, warmed serving dish. Dish the boiling broth into the serving dish, sprinkle spring onions, coriander and pepper on top and serve at once. The boiling broth will cook the fish slices.

Chicken Broth

Preparation time 30–40 min • Cooking time 2 hr • Serves 4

Chicken 1/2 (about 900 g)
Water 10 cups
Salt 1 1/2 tsp
Rice 1/2 cup
Ginger 6 slices, finely shredded
Spring onions 2, chopped
A shake of pepper

1. Clean the chicken. Heat water in a big pot and when it boils, put in the chicken. Turn the heat very low and simmer for 30 minutes. Remove the chicken and debone it. Return bones to the pot of stock. Cut chicken meat into 1-cm strips and season with 1/2 tsp salt.

2. Wash the rice and put into stock to cook. When rice is soft, simmer for a few more minutes before turning off heat. If a very soft, thick broth is desired, simmer till rice grains are broken, adding more boiling hot water if necessary.

3. When broth is ready, remove the chicken bones and add the remaining salt or to taste. Place chicken pieces with ginger strips in a large warmed serving dish. Dish hot broth over the chicken, sprinkle spring onions and pepper on top and serve at once.

Note: As an added garnishing for the three types of broth, deep-fry 1/4 piece of dried rice vermicelli (*mee hoon*) till light brown, puffy and crispy. Sprinkle fried vermicelli on top of broth just before serving.

Meat

Satay

Satay

Preparation time 1¹/₂–2 hr • Cooking time 10 min

Beef or chicken 500 g
Shallots 10
Lemon grass (*serai*) 3 stalks
Galangal (*lengkuas*) 1 thin slice
Ginger 2.5-cm knob
Ground coriander ¹/₂ Tbsp
Ground aniseed ¹/₂ tsp
Ground cumin 1 tsp
Sugar ¹/₂ cup
Salt 1 tsp
Turmeric powder 1 tsp
Coconut ¹/₂ cup, grated
Cooking oil ¹/₄ cup

1. Cut the meat into thin bite-sized pieces. Grind shallots, lemon grass, galangal and ginger to a smooth paste. Mix this paste with the ground spices, sugar, salt and turmeric powder. Marinate the meat in this mixture for at least 1 hour before threading on thin satay skewers. The meat can be kept refrigerated overnight in this marinade.

2. Extract ¹/₄ cup coconut milk from grated coconut. Mix the cooking oil with the coconut milk and use this for basting the meat while grilling.

3. Make a charcoal fire in a charcoal brazier. Use a rectangular tin with metal grating or wire toaster over the open top if you do not have a proper charcoal brazier. When ready to start the meal, grill skewered meat over the charcoal fire, basting with the oil and coconut milk mixture till the meat is cooked. If you have a barbecue pit or a few braziers, yours guests can join in the fun.

4. Serve with *satay sauce, onion and cucumber wedges, and Lontong (page 17) or toast.

*Satay Sauce

Shallots 12–15
Galangal (*lengkuas*) 2 thin slices
Ginger 2-cm knob
Lemon grass (*serai*) 1 stalk
Peanuts 450 g, roasted
Tamarind pulp 2 Tbsp
Water ¹/₂ cup
Cooking oil ¹/₂ cup
Red chillies 1 Tbsp, ground
Palm sugar (*gula Melaka*) 10 Tbsp, chopped
Salt 1 tsp

1. Grind shallots, galangal, ginger and lemon grass. Crush roasted peanuts either with a rolling pin, in a mortar or in a blender. Extract ¹/₂ cup tamarind juice from tamarind and water.

2. Heat cooking oil and fry the ground chillies and other ground ingredients till the oil separates from the ingredients. Add crushed peanuts and mix well before adding chopped palm sugar, salt and tamarind juice. Stir the mixture and allow it to simmer until the gravy is thick and the oil rises to the top.

Note: This sauce can be kept refrigerated for a few days. Leftover sauce is delicious with rice, potatoes or sliced cucumber.

**Lemon Grass
(*Serai* or *Heong Mow*)**

A tall grass with very fleshy leaf bases that are used for flavouring food, especially curries. Use only 10–12 cm of the slightly swollen leaf bases. When sliced and dried, they keep very well. Fresh lemon grass is available from the market.

Mui Choy Chee Yoke
(Pork with Preserved Spinach)

Preparation time 30 min • *Cooking time* 2 hr • *Serves* 6–8

Belly pork 500 g
Light soy sauce 2 Tbsp
Cooking oil for deep-frying
Cooking oil 1 Tbsp
Preserved spinach (*mui choy*) 100 g
Shallots 3, sliced
Ginger 3 slices
Dark soy sauce 1 Tbsp
Sugar 1 Tbsp
Rice wine 1 Tbsp
Salt 1 tsp

1. Clean and cut pork into large pieces about 7.5-cm wide. It is best to buy a strip 7.5-cm wide and cut it into two. Put pork in a pan with enough water to cover and cook for 30 minutes. Remove and drain. Keep the stock aside. Puncture skin all over with a skewer, dab skin dry with a clean cloth and rub light soy sauce all over skin.

2. Heat cooking oil for deep-frying. Place pork into hot oil with skin side down and fry for 3–5 minutes until skin is golden brown. To prevent oil from splattering, cover the pan while frying. Remove pork from oil and cool it. When cool enough to handle, cut pork into 1-cm thick pieces. Arrange pieces of pork skin side downwards in a Chinese soup bowl or any heatproof bowl. Pack slices tightly together.

3. Soak and wash preserved spinach to remove excess salt and squeeze dry. Cut it into 0.25-cm strips. Heat a clean dry wok and fry preserved spinach over medium heat for 5–7 minutes to remove some of the vegetable's strong flavour, which may be offensive to some.

4. Heat 1 Tbsp cooking oil and fry shallots and ginger till lightly browned. Add preserved spinach and toss it in the oil. Add the reserved stock, mixed with dark soy sauce, sugar, rice wine and salt. Cover the pan and let it simmer for about 5 minutes.

5. Spoon the mixture over the pork slices. Put bowl in a steamer and steam for 1–1½ hours over boiling water. Invert bowl onto a warmed serving dish and serve hot.

Shredded Pork with Szechuan Vegetable

Preparation time 25 min • *Cooking time* 15–20 min • *Serves* 4–6

Lean pork 300 g
Salt ½ tsp
Tapioca flour 1 tsp
Rice wine 1 tsp
Water 3 Tbsp
Sesame oil ½ tsp
Pepper ¼ tsp
Cooking oil for deep-frying
Shallots 4, sliced
Ginger 2.5-cm knob, shredded
Szechuan vegetable ½ cup, shredded and soaked
Capsicum 1, shredded
Bamboo shoot ½ cup, boiled and shredded
Carrot 1 small, boiled and shredded
Spring onion 1, cut into 4-cm lengths

1. Shred pork and marinate it in a mixture of salt, ½ tsp tapioca flour, rice wine and 1 Tbsp water.

2. For the gravy, mix the remaining water and tapioca flour, sesame oil, and pepper.

3. Heat cooking oil for deep-frying. When oil is hot, fry seasoned pork for 1 minute till it changes colour. Remove and drain well.

4. Remove all but ½ Tbsp cooking oil from the pan, heat it and brown shallots and ginger. Add Szechuan vegetable and capsicum and fry for 1–2 minutes. Add bamboo shoot, carrot and pork and toss all together. Finally, add gravy mixture and spring onion and toss together for another minute. Season to taste and serve.

Shredded Pork with Szechuan Vegetable

Minced Pork Steamed with Mushrooms

Minced Pork Steamed with Mushrooms

Preparation time 15 min • *Cooking time* 30 min • *Serves 6–8*

Dried Chinese mushrooms 6–8,
  soaked to soften
Light soy sauce 1 Tbsp
Tapioca flour 2 Tbsp
Pork 300 g, minced
Salt 1/2 tsp
A shake of pepper
Water 2 Tbsp

1. Clean mushrooms, remove stems and chop finely. Season chopped mushrooms with soy sauce and 1 Tbsp tapioca flour. Mix them well together.

2. Put minced pork in a bowl, then add the remaining tapioca flour, salt and a good shake of pepper and knead them well together. While kneading, gradually add water. When pork is well kneaded and tacky, knead in mushrooms. Place pork mixture in a heatproof dish and steam over boiling water for 30 minutes. Serve hot.

Note: Instead of mushrooms, use either dried squid, preserved cabbage (*tong choy*) or preserved turnip (*tai tow choy*). This dish can also be steamed by placing it on top of the rice in a rice cooker, just when the rice is drying up. It will be cooked when the rice is cooked.

Tow Cheong Chee Yoke
(Shredded Pork with Preserved Soy Bean Paste)

Preparation time 15 min • *Cooking time* 15 min • *Serves 4–6*

Pork 300 g
Light soy sauce 1 tsp
Tapioca flour 2 tsp
Rice wine 1 1/2 tsp
Cooking oil for deep-frying
Preserved soy beans (*tow cheong*)
  1 Tbsp, mashed
Sugar 2 tsp
Bird's eye chillies (*cili padi*)
  (optional) 2, sliced thickly
Water 2 Tbsp
Spring onion 1, cut into 4-cm lengths

1. Clean and shred pork thinly. Season it with a mixture of soy sauce, tapioca flour and 1 tsp rice wine. Leave it in the marinade for 30 minutes.

2. Heat cooking oil for deep-frying and fry pork over a slow heat for 2–3 minutes until cooked. Remove from oil and drain.

3. Remove all but 1/2 Tbsp cooking oil from the pan, heat it and fry preserved soy bean paste for 2–3 minutes. Add sugar, bird's eye chillies (optional) and water. When gravy boils, add the remaining rice wine and fried pork and mix thoroughly. Finally, mix in chopped spring onion, season to taste and serve.

Barbecued Spareribs

Preparation time 5 min • *Cooking time* 30–40 min • *Serves 4*

Spareribs 600 g
A few slices of cucumber

MARINADE
Preserved soy beans (*tow cheong*)
    1 Tbsp, mashed
Hoisin sauce (*teem cheong*) 1 Tbsp
Sweet plum sauce 1 Tbsp
Red fermented bean curd 1 piece
Five spice powder (*ng heong fun*) $^1/_2$ tsp
Rice wine 1 Tbsp
Sugar 3 Tbsp

1. Combine marinade ingredients and season the spareribs for at least 2 hours, turning them over every 30 minutes.

2. Heat the oven to 230°C. Remove the spareribs from the marinade and place in a roasting pan. Bake for 30 minutes, basting with the marinade every 10 minutes or till meat is cooked and brown. If meat browns too quickly, lower the oven temperature, or switch off after 20 minutes, cover the meat with tin foil and allow meat to continue cooking in the hot oven. If no oven is available, cook the ribs under a grill or over a charcoal fire, cooking each side for not less than 15 minutes.

3. Cut ribs apart and serve them garnished with sliced cucumber.

Char Siew
(Chinese BBQ Pork)

Preparation time 10 min • *Cooking time* 25–30 min • *Serves 6–8*

Pork shoulder 600 g
Fish sauce 3 Tbsp
Dark soy sauce $^1/_2$ Tbsp
Sugar 3 Tbsp
Rice wine 1 Tbsp

1. Cut pork into long strips 3–4-cm thick. Marinate with fish sauce, dark soy sauce, sugar and rice wine and leave for at least 2 hours. Turn meat over every 30 minutes.

2. Heat the grill, put seasoned pork strips into the pan and grill slowly for about 15 minutes on each side. Brush seasoning sauce on the pork strips every 5 minutes. (If no grill is available, heat 1 Tbsp cooking oil in a frying pan and fry the strips till cooked and brown).

3. The seasoning sauce can be cooked in a pan till it is thick and poured over the sliced BBQ pork before serving.

Char Siew (Chinese BBQ Pork)

Sweet Sour Pork

Sweet Sour Pork

Preparation time 30 min • Cooking time 25–30 min • Serves 4–6

Lean pork shoulder 300 g
Salt 1 tsp
Sugar 2 tsp
A shake of pepper
Egg 1, beaten
Cornflour 4 Tbsp
Cucumber 1
Onion 1
Tomatoes 2
Capsicum 1
Spring onion 1
Vinegar $^1/_2$ Tbsp
Tomato ketchup 2 Tbsp
Chilli sauce (optional) 1 tsp
Sesame oil $^1/_2$ tsp
Water $^1/_2$ cup
Cooking oil for deep-frying
Cornflour $^1/_2$ Tbsp, blended with
    2 Tbsp water

1. Clean and cut pork into 3-cm squares, 1-cm thick. Season pork with $^1/_2$ tsp salt, $^1/_2$ tsp sugar and pepper. Knead the beaten egg well into the pork and then mix in 2 Tbsp cornflour and leave pork to season for at least 30 minutes.

2. Skin cucumber, quarter it lengthwise, remove the soft centre, and cut each quarter into 2-cm lengths. Cut onion into segments, quarter tomatoes, remove seeds from capsicum and cut into irregular 2-cm pieces. Cut spring onion into 2-cm lengths. Mix together the remaining salt and sugar, vinegar, tomato ketchup, chilli sauce (optional) and sesame oil with water for gravy.

3. Heat cooking oil for deep-frying. Roll seasoned pork pieces in some dry cornflour and fry in hot oil till cooked and crisp. Drain off oil and set aside.

4. Remove oil from the pan. Fry onion segments for one minute in the oily pan before adding the gravy mixture. When gravy boils, add the capsicum, tomatoes and cucumber pieces. Thicken gravy with cornflour mixture. Season to taste, then add in the fried pork pieces. Turn off heat at once. Add the spring onion, mix well and serve immediately.

Sweet Sour Spareribs

Preparation time 15 min • Cooking time 25 min • Serves 4

Spareribs 600 g
Garlic 3 cloves, chopped finely
Salt 1 tsp
Dark soy sauce $^1/_2$ tsp
Rice wine 1 Tbsp
Pepper $^1/_4$ tsp
Tomato ketchup 1 Tbsp
Worcestershire sauce 1 Tbsp
Sesame oil $^1/_2$ tsp
Sugar $^1/_2$ Tbsp
Water 2 Tbsp
Cooking oil for deep-frying
Tapioca flour 3 Tbsp
Tomato 1, sliced

1. Clean and cut spareribs into finger-length pieces. Season ribs with garlic, salt, dark soy sauce, rice wine and pepper. Leave to marinate for 1 hour. Mix together tomato ketchup, Worcestershire sauce, sesame oil, sugar and water for the gravy. Set aside.

2. Heat cooking oil for deep-frying. Turn down heat, coat the ribs with tapioca flour and fry for 5 minutes. Remove from the oil. Reheat oil till smoking hot and re-fry the ribs for another minute. Remove and drain.

3. Remove all oil from the pan, pour in the well-mixed gravy ingredients and let it boil till thick. Add the fried ribs, toss to mix well and serve garnished with tomato slices.

Yuen Tai

(Stewed Pork Shoulder)

Preparation time 20 min • *Cooking time* 1³/₄–2 hr • *Serves* 6–8

Pork shoulder or thigh 500 g
Water 2 cups
Cooking oil 2 Tbsp
Szechuan pepper (*fah chew*) 1 tsp
Fish sauce 1¹/₂ tsp
Oyster sauce 1 Tbsp
Dark soy sauce 1 Tbsp
Rock sugar 1 thumb-sized piece
Chinese wine 1 tsp

1. Clean meat and tie it into a neat roll. Heat water in a pan. When water boils put roll of meat in for about 10 minutes, turning constantly so that all parts are immersed in boiling water for a little while.

2. Take out partially cooked meat and keep the stock for later use. Heat cooking oil in a pan, put in meat and turn it in the oil till it is well coated. Add the stock and the Szechuan pepper, which has been tied in a piece of muslin, and boil for 10 minutes.

3. Add the fish sauce and allow meat to simmer slowly for 1¹/₂ hours. When meat is tender, add the oyster sauce, dark soy sauce, rock sugar and Chinese wine. Season to taste and serve the meat whole on a bed of boiled green vegetables, such as flowering cabbage (*choy sum*) or lettuce, on a warmed serving dish.

Note: Szechuan pepper (*fah chew*) is a spice obtainable from Chinese medicine shops. For Chinese wine, you may use Siew Hing wine or any Chinese cooking wine, obtainable from the supermarket.

Spring Rolls

Preparation time 30 min • *Cooking time* 15–20 min

Pork 150 g
Water chestnuts 6
Onion ¹/₂, large
Mushrooms 4
Prawns 225 g, shelled and deveined
Crabmeat (optional) 2 Tbsp
Tapioca flour 6 Tbsp
Salt ¹/₂ tsp
A shake of pepper
Sesame oil 2 tsp
Five spice powder (*ng heong fun*) ¹/₄ tsp
Egg 1, beaten
Mysentery (pig's caul) or dried bean curd sheet (*fu pei*) 150 g
Cooking oil for deep-frying
Cucumber and tomato slices
Limes 2, wedged

1. Clean and cut pork into 0.5-cm strips. Dice water chestnuts, onion and mushrooms.

2. Chop up prawns. Mix pork, water chestnuts, onion, mushrooms, prawns and crabmeat (optional) with 1 tsp tapioca flour, salt, pepper, sesame oil, five spice powder and egg.

3. Clean mysentery, if using, and cut into 20-cm squares.

4. Place portions of filling on pieces of mysentery or dried bean curd sheets and roll each piece into a neat, tight roll. For mysentery rolls, coat with tapioca flour. For dried bean curd sheet rolls, seal the edges with tapioca flour paste. Deep-fry till golden brown.

5. Drain well, cut into 2.5-cm pieces and serve garnished with cucumber and tomato slices and lime wedges. Serve with *spiced salt.

*Spiced Salt

Salt 2 Tbsp
Five spice powder (*ng heong fun*) 1 tsp

1. Combine ingredients in a clean, dry pan, stirring continuously. Fry over low heat for 3–4 minutes. Keep spiced salt in an airtight jar and use when needed.

Beef in Clay Pot

Preparation time 10 min • *Cooking time* 30 min • *Serves* 6–8

Shallots 6
Garlic 1 head
Ginger 1-cm knob
Coriander leaves 2 sprigs
Belly beef 600 g
Peppercorns 10
Light soy sauce 1 Tbsp
Five spice powder (*ng heong fun*) $^1/_4$ tsp
Water 1 cup
Cooking oil 1 Tbsp
Sesame oil 1 tsp
Oyster sauce 2 Tbsp
Dark soy sauce 1 Tbsp
Cornflour 2 tsp, blended with 1 Tbsp water
Rice wine 1 Tbsp

1. Skin shallots, wash and leave them whole. Separate cloves of garlic. Skin and wash them and leave them whole. Slice ginger, chop coriander leaves for garnishing but keep the roots for cooking.

2. Place beef, coriander roots, peppercorns, light soy sauce and five spice powder in a pan with water and allow it to simmer slowly. When meat is tender, drain and cut it up into 5-cm square pieces. Keep stock aside.

3. Heat cooking oil with sesame oil in a clay pot and fry shallots, garlic and ginger till they are limp. Add reserved stock, oyster sauce and dark soy sauce. When it boils, add the meat and cook for another 10 minutes. Thicken the gravy with cornflour mixture. Season to taste and turn off heat. Mix in rice wine and serve garnished with coriander leaves.

Note: If desired, add some Chinese celery (*kun choy*) to the beef for the last 10 minutes of cooking time.

Chinese Beef Steak

Preparation time 10 min • *Cooking time* 8 min • *Serves* 6

STEAK
Fillet steak 500 g
Salt $^1/_2$ tsp
Sugar $^1/_2$ tsp
Bicarbonate of soda 1 tsp
Light soy sauce 1$^1/_2$ tsp
Tapioca flour 2 Tbsp
Egg 1, small, beaten
Water 6 Tbsp
Worcestershire sauce 1 Tbsp
Cooking oil 5 Tbsp

GRAVY
Water $^1/_4$ cup
Salt $^1/_4$ tsp
Sugar 3 tsp
Worcestershire sauce 1 Tbsp
Tomato ketchup 1 Tbsp
Sesame oil $^1/_2$ tsp
Pepper $^1/_4$ tsp

STEAK

1. Clean fillet steak and cut it into 12–14 pieces, cutting across the grain. Using the back of a chopper, pound the pieces of meat on both sides to tenderise.

2. Marinate the meat in a mixture of salt, sugar, bicarbonate of soda, light soy sauce, tapioca flour and egg. Knead meat for at least 5 minutes, adding water gradually. Lastly, add Worcestershire sauce and 2 Tbsp cooking oil and knead once again. Leave the meat in the marinade for at least 3 hours.

GRAVY

3. Mix thoroughly water, salt, sugar, Worcestershire sauce, tomato ketchup, sesame oil and pepper. Set aside.

4. Heat the remaining cooking oil in a frying pan. Fry the steak 6 pieces at a time over high heat. When one side is done, turn over to fry the other side. Each side should not take more than1 minute. Remove the pieces of steak from the pan when they are about half cooked.

5. In the same pan, cook the gravy mixture, stirring until it boils. Allow the gravy to boil for 2–3 minutes before returning the pieces of steak to the pan. Toss well to mix so that the pieces of steak are evenly coated with gravy. Serve at once.

Fried Beef with Oyster Sauce

Preparation time 15 min • *Cooking time* 12 min • *Serves* 4–6

Fillet steak 300 g
Bicarbonate of soda $^1/_4$ tsp
Salt 1 tsp
Sugar 1 tsp
Light soy sauce 2 tsp
Dark soy sauce 1 tsp
Sesame oil 1 tsp
Tapioca flour 1$^1/_2$ Tbsp
Pepper $^1/_4$ tsp
Water 7 Tbsp
Cooking oil for marinade
    and deep-frying
Ginger 1-cm knob
Spring onion 1
Carrot 1, small
Oyster sauce 2 tsp
Rice wine $^1/_2$ Tbsp

1. Clean and slice beef very thinly across the grain. Season beef with bicarbonate of soda, $^1/_2$ tsp salt, $^1/_2$ tsp sugar, 1 tsp light soy sauce, dark soy sauce, $^1/_2$ tsp sesame oil, 1 Tbsp tapioca flour and a good shake of pepper. Knead beef thoroughly, gradually adding 2 Tbsp water. Lastly, knead in $^1/_2$ Tbsp cooking oil and allow meat to marinate for 30 minutes.

2. Clean and slice ginger thinly. Cut spring onion into 4-cm lengths and carrot into 0.25-cm slices or fancy shapes.

3. Mix ingredients for gravy: mix together the remaining water, salt, sugar, light soy sauce, sesame oil and tapioca flour together with oyster sauce and a good shake of pepper.

4. Heat 3 cups cooking oil for deep-frying. When oil is very hot, put in seasoned beef and remove pan from heat. Fry beef for $^1/_2$ minute then remove it from the pan. Drain well.

5. Remove all but $^1/_2$ Tbsp cooking oil from the pan. Fry the ginger slices and carrot. Add the beef and the well mixed gravy mixture. As soon as it boils, add the spring onion and rice wine. Season to taste and serve.

Fried Beef with Spring Onion

Preparation time 15–20 min • *Cooking time* 8 min • *Serves* 4–6

Fillet steak 300 g
Salt 1 tsp
Light soy sauce 1 tsp
A shake of pepper
Tapioca flour 1 Tbsp
Bicarbonate of soda $^1/_4$ tsp
Young ginger 7.5-cm knob
Spring onion 150 g
Egg 1
Cooking oil 1 Tbsp
Water $^1/_2$ cup
Rice wine (optional) 1 Tbsp

1. Clean and slice beef very thinly across the grain. Season beef with salt, soy sauce, pepper, tapioca flour and bicarbonate of soda. Knead thoroughly to mix well.

2. Clean and slice ginger thinly. Rub a little salt into the ginger and wash away the salt after 10 minutes. Clean and cut spring onion into 4-cm lengths. Beat the egg with a good shake of pepper.

3. Heat cooking oil and lightly fry ginger for 1 minute. Add beef, spring onion and water, and without stirring, cover the pan to cook for 3 minutes. Toss the ingredients together to mix after 3 minutes. Turn off the heat as soon as the ingredients are mixed and the beef has changed colour. Make a well in the centre of the ingredients and pour in the beaten egg. Mix well and serve at once. If desired, add 1 Tbsp rice wine just before serving.

Fried Beef with Spring Onion

Braised Beef with Radish

Preparation time 15 min • Cooking time 1½ hr • Serves 6–8

Shin beef 300 g
Radish 1
Cooking oil 1½ Tbsp
Garlic 1 clove, sliced
Ginger 1 slice
Onion 1, large, quartered
Water 2 cups
Star anise 1 segment
Peppercorns 6
Light soy sauce 4 Tbsp
Sugar ½ Tbsp
Salt ½ tsp
Coriander leaves 1 sprig, chopped

1. Clean and cut beef into 4-cm cubes. Cut radish into pieces about the size of the meat.

2. Heat cooking oil and brown garlic, ginger and onion lightly. Add beef and toss it in oil to seal in the juices. Add water, star anise, peppercorns, soy sauce, sugar and salt and simmer in a covered pan for 2 hours.

3. When beef is tender, add radish and cook for another 30 minutes or until radish is tender. Season to taste and serve garnished with coriander leaves.

Beef Kurmah

(Mild Beef Curry)

Preparation time 30 min • Cooking time 1½ hr • Serves 6–8

Beef 600 g
Coriander 2 Tbsp
Cumin 1 Tbsp
Aniseed 1 dsp
Peppercorns 1 dsp
Almonds 20
Coconut ¾, grated
Cooking oil or ghee 3 Tbsp
Shallots 16, sliced
Garlic 2 cloves, sliced
Ginger 1-cm knob, shredded
Cinnamon stick 5-cm length
Cloves 3
Cardamom 3 pods
Lemon grass (*serai*) 1 stalk, bruised
Salt 1 tsp
Lime juice extracted from 1 lime

1. Clean and cut beef into 1-cm thick pieces. Grind or pound together coriander, cumin, aniseed and peppercorns. Grind or pound almonds separately. Extract ½ cup first coconut milk and 1½ cups second coconut milk from grated coconut.

2. Heat cooking oil or ghee in a pan and fry shallots, garlic and ginger until light brown. Add cinnamon, cloves, cardamoms, lemon grass and ground spices.

3. Add meat and salt and toss until meat is sealed all over. Stir in the second extraction (1½ cups) of coconut milk, cover the pan and simmer until meat is tender.

4. When meat is tender, add the first extraction (½ cup) of coconut milk and the ground almonds and continue cooking till gravy is of the right consistency. Add lime juice and season to taste.

Note: This is a white curry. It is not pungent but very rich. The following substitutions may be made for this recipe: chicken for beef, candlenuts for almonds, yoghurt for coconut milk (though in this case the flavour would not be quite the same). Onions and tomatoes can also be added to the curry with the almonds.

Beef Rendang

Preparation time 30 min • *Cooking time* 1¹/₂–2 hr • *Serves 6–8*

Shin beef 600 g
Dried red chillies 15–20, soaked
    to soften
Shallots 20
Galangal (*lengkuas*) 1-cm knob
Lemon grass (*serai*) 5 stalks
Coconuts 2, grated
Dried sour fruit (*asam gelugur*)
    3 slices
Salt 1 tsp
Turmeric leaf 1, torn into pieces

1. Clean and cut beef into 1-cm thick pieces. Grind or pound chillies, shallots, galangal and lemon grass. Extract 4 cups of coconut milk from grated coconut.

2. Put meat, ground ingredients and coconut milk into a wok and bring it to boil. Quickly lower the heat to allow ingredients to simmer. Stir mixture every 10 minutes to prevent burning. Simmer till meat is tender and gravy is reduced and thick.

3. When the meat is nearly done, add dried sour fruit slices and salt and cook until the curry is almost dry. Add the turmeric leaf. Continue cooking till the curry is dry enough, stirring all the while to prevent burning. Season to taste.

Beef Curry

Preparation time 25 min • Cooking time 1¹/₂–2 hr • Serves 6–8

Beef 600 g
Coconut ¹/₂, grated
Cooking oil 2 Tbsp
Cloves 3
Cinnamon stick 5-cm length
Cardamom 2 pods
Star anise 2 segments
Cumin 1 tsp
Ginger 2.5-cm knob, shredded
Shallots 10, sliced
Curry leaves 1 sprig
Curry powder 2 Tbsp
Green chillies 4, slit into 4 at the tip
Potatoes 4, cubed
Salt 1 tsp
Lime 1

1. Clean and cut beef into 5-cm square pieces of 1-cm thickness. Extract ¹/₂ cup first coconut milk and 1¹/₂ cups second coconut milk from grated coconut.

2. Heat the cooking oil and fry cloves, cinnamon, cardamom, star anise and cumin for 1 minute. Add ginger, shallots and curry leaves and fry for another 2 minutes. Add meat and fry for a few minutes to seal in the juices. Add the second extraction (1¹/₂ cups) of coconut milk and cook till meat is tender.

3. When meat is tender, add curry powder, green chillies and potatoes and cook till curry is thick. Stir frequently to prevent burning. Add the first extraction (¹/₂ cup) of coconut milk and salt and cook curry till it is as thick as desired. Squeeze lime juice into the curry and season to taste. Serve with rice or bread.

Note: Fry curry powder in a clean, dry frying pan over low heat for 5 minutes before use. This will make the curry more fragrant.

Poultry

Duck Stewed with Ginger

Duck Stewed with Ginger

Preparation time 40 min • *Cooking time* 25–30 min • *Serves* 6–8

Duck 1 (about 1.5 kg)
Light soy sauce 2 Tbsp
Dark soy sauce 2 tsp
Dried Chinese mushrooms 6, soaked
Young ginger 75 g
Garlic 2 cloves
Spring onions 2
Lettuce 300 g
Preserved soy beans
    (*tow cheong*) 1/2 Tbsp
Water 4 cups
Salt 1/2 tsp
Sugar 1 tsp
Sesame oil 2 tsp
A shake of pepper
Cooking oil for deep-frying
Tapioca flour 1 Tbsp, blended with
    2 Tbsp water
Rice wine 1 Tbsp

1. Clean duck and cut it into about 24 small pieces. Season with 1 Tbsp light soy sauce and 1 tsp dark soy sauce.

2. Remove stems from mushrooms and halve or quarter each, depending on size. Cut the ginger into 0.5-cm slices. Chop the garlic. Cut spring onions into 4-cm lengths and clean lettuce leaves. Mash preserved soy beans.

3. Mix gravy ingredients: add salt, sugar, sesame oil, pepper, the remaining light and dark soy sauce to the water. Mix well.

4. Heat cooking oil for deep-frying and fry duck until pieces are brown in colour. Take out browned duck and remove all but 1 Tbsp oil.

5. In the hot oil, brown garlic and ginger. Then add the preserved soy bean paste and stir-fry for 1 minute. Add the fried duck, mushrooms and gravy mixture. Cover the pan and simmer for at least 1 hour over very low heat. When meat is tender, boil quickly to reduce gravy. Thicken gravy with tapioca flour mixture. Season to taste. Finally, add rice wine and spring onion. Boil lettuce and arrange on serving plate. Serve stewed duck on bed of boiled lettuce.

Teochew Duck

Preparation time 15 min • *Cooking time* 1 3/4 hr • *Serves* 6–8

Duck 1 (about 1.5 kg)
Galangal (*lengkuas*) 2.5-cm knob
Cooking oil 4 Tbsp
Sugar 3 Tbsp
Light soy sauce 2 Tbsp
Dark soy sauce 1 Tbsp
Water 3 cups

1. Clean duck and cut off the legs. Slice galangal into four, stuff the slices into the duck and dry the duck.

2. Heat cooking oil in a pan and add sugar to it. Stir sugar in the oil till it forms a dark caramel. Put duck into the pan and turn it about until it is evenly browned by the caramel. Add light and dark soy sauce and continue turning the duck in it. When the duck is evenly coated, add water, cover the pan and allow duck to simmer for 1 1/2 hours until it is tender and the gravy is thick. If there is too much gravy, boil quickly for 2–3 minutes to reduce it. Season to taste. Cut into bite-sized pieces and serve.

Note: A strip of belly or shoulder pork can be cooked with the duck and served together with it. Compliment this dish with *chilli sauce.

*Chilli Sauce

Red chillies 10
Garlic 3 cloves
Vinegar 4–5 Tbsp
Salt 1/2 tsp
Sugar to taste

1. Pound chillies and garlic and mix in vinegar, salt and sugar to get a sauce of the consistency desired.

Mild Chicken Curry

Preparation time 40 min • *Cooking time* 40 min • *Serves* 6–8

Chicken 1 (about 1.5 kg)
Dried red chillies 15, soaked to soften
Lemon grass (*serai*) 2 stalks
Fresh turmeric (*kunyit*) 1-cm knob
Galangal (*lengkuas*) 2.5-cm knob
Shallots 15
Garlic 2 cloves
Candlenuts (*buah keras*) 4
Dried shrimp paste (*belacan*)
    2.5 x 2.5 x 0.5-cm piece
Coconut 1, grated
Cooking oil 3 Tbsp
Salt 1$\frac{1}{2}$ tsp
Kaffir lime leaves (*daun limau purut*)
    (optional) 10

1. Clean chicken and cut into 12–14 pieces. Pound together chillies, lemon grass, turmeric, galangal, shallots, garlic, candlenuts and dried shrimp paste. Extract 1 cup first coconut milk and 2 cups second coconut milk from the grated coconut.

2. Heat cooking oil and fry ground spices until well cooked and fragrant before adding the chicken pieces. Add the second extraction (2 cups) of coconut milk, cover the pan and simmer for about 30 minutes until chicken is tender.

3. When the chicken is tender and curry gravy is thick, add the first extraction (1 cup) of coconut milk and kaffir lime leaves, if desired, stirring gently for about 3 minutes or until curry is thick and has a thin layer of oil on top. Season to taste and if preferred, squeeze some lime juice in before serving.

Chicken Curry

Preparation time 40 min • *Cooking time* 30–40 min • *Serves* 6–8

Coconut $\frac{1}{2}$, grated
Garlic 8 cloves
Ginger 2.5-cm knob
Chicken 1 (about 1.5 kg)
Ground chilli 1 Tbsp
Curry powder 2 Tbsp
Salt 1 tsp
Cooking oil 2 Tbsp
Curry leaves 1 sprig, or 1 bay leaf
Shallots 8, sliced
Lime 1

1. Extract 1 cup first coconut milk and 2 cups second coconut milk from grated coconut. Pound together garlic and ginger. Clean the chicken and cut it into 12–15 pieces. Season with ground chilli, curry powder, pounded ginger and garlic, followed by salt.

2. Heat cooking oil in a pan and fry curry or bay leaves and shallots until shallots are limp. Add seasoned chicken and fry to seal in the juices. Add the second extraction (2 cups) of coconut milk and stir till well mixed. Cover the pan and allow curry to simmer for $\frac{1}{2}$ hour till chicken is tender.

3. When chicken is tender and curry is fairly thick, add the first extraction (1 cup) of coconut milk and a squeeze of lime juice from the lime. Season to taste.

Chicken Curry

Ayam Golek (Roast Chicken)

Ayam Golek

(Roast Chicken)

Preparation time 40–50 min • *Cooking time* 1 hr • *Serves* 6–8

Dried red chillies 15, soaked to soften
Shallots 5
Garlic 2 cloves
Ginger 1-cm knob
Galangal (*lengkuas*) 1-cm knob
Salt 1$\frac{1}{2}$ tsp
Lemon grass (*serai*) 1 stalk
Chicken 1 (about 1.5 kg)
Water $\frac{1}{2}$ cup
Coconuts 1$\frac{1}{2}$, grated
Sugar 2 tsp

1. Grind together chillies, shallots, garlic, ginger, galangal and salt. Bruise lemon grass by lightly pounding it. Clean chicken and rub a little of the ground ingredients all over it. Put lemon grass into the cavity of the chicken. Place the chicken in a roasting tin and bake at 200°C.

2. Add water to grated coconut and extract thick coconut milk. Put the rest of the ground ingredients and coconut milk in a saucepan. Add sugar and cook, stirring all the time until the mixture thickens.

3. After 30 minutes in the oven, baste the chicken with the coconut mixture. Return chicken to the oven. Repeat basting every 5 minutes until chicken is tender and the coconut mixture is used up. Before serving the chicken, pour gravy from the roasting tin all over it.

Chicken Casserole

Preparation time 20 min • *Cooking time* 40–50 min • *Serves* 4

Chicken thighs 8
Salt 1 tsp
A shake of pepper
Onion 1
Button mushrooms 1 can, reserve brine
Cooking oil 8 Tbsp
Tomato puree 4 Tbsp
Cornflour 1 Tbsp
Sugar $\frac{1}{2}$ tsp
Sherry 1 Tbsp

1. Clean chicken thighs and season them with salt and pepper. Dice the onion and halve button mushrooms.

2. Heat cooking oil and brown each piece of chicken before putting it in the casserole. Remove the remaining oil and lightly brown the diced onion in the oily pan. Add tomato purée, cornflour, salt, sugar and pepper, well mixed with 1 cup of the mushroom brine. When gravy boils and thickens, add the mushrooms and sherry. Then pour gravy over the chicken in the casserole.

3. Cover the casserole and cook it in a moderate oven (190°C) for 40 minutes until chicken is tender. Serve casserole with boiled green peas or carrots and buttered rice or riced potatoes.

Note: To make buttered rice, boil rice in the usual way. Mix butter with the hot rice before serving. To make riced potatoes, boil potatoes. When potatoes are cooked, peel them and put them through the potato ricer.

Steamed Chicken with Sausage

Preparation time 15–20 min • *Cooking time* 20–30 min • *Serves* 4–6

Chicken meat 2 cups
Ginger 4-cm knob
Tapioca flour 2 Tbsp
Light soy sauce 2 Tbsp
A shake of pepper
Chinese sausages 1 pair
Dried Chinese mushrooms 4, soaked
Salt $1/2$ tsp
Rice wine 1 Tbsp
Coriander leaves 1 sprig, chopped

1. Cut chicken meat into bite-sized portions. Pound ginger and squeeze for juice. Season chicken with 1 Tbsp tapioca flour, 1 Tbsp light soy sauce, ginger juice and pepper.

2. Slice sausage, wash and quarter mushrooms. Season mushrooms with the remaining tapioca flour and light soy sauce together with salt.

3. Mix seasoned chicken with sausages and seasoned mushrooms and add rice wine and pepper. Place the ingredients in a heatproof dish and steam over boiling water for 20 minutes. Serve garnished with coriander leaves.

Note: To make buttered rice, boil rice in the usual way. Mix butter with the hot rice before serving. To make riced potatoes, boil potatoes. When potatoes are cooked, peel them and put them through the potato ricer.

Chicken Legs Stewed with Mushrooms

Preparation time 20 min • *Cooking time* 40–50 min • *Serves* 4

Chicken legs 10
Light soy sauce $1 1/2$ Tbsp
Cooking oil for marinade and deep-frying
Dried Chinese mushrooms 20, soaked
Tapioca flour 2 tsp
Chinese cabbage 6 leaves
Chicken stock 2 cups
Salt $3/4$ tsp
Sugar 1 tsp
Oyster sauce 1 tsp
Sesame oil $1/2$ tsp
A shake of pepper
Ginger 1-cm knob, sliced
Shallots 2, sliced
Garlic 2 cloves, sliced

1. Season chicken legs with 1 Tbsp light soy sauce. Heat cooking oil for deep-frying and fry chicken legs until brown. Remove from hot oil and put into a pan of cold water. Halve each leg.

2. Remove stems from mushrooms. Halve and season with tapioca flour, 1 tsp light soy sauce and 1 Tbsp cooking oil. Clean and cut Chinese cabbage into 5-cm lengths.

3. Mix gravy ingredients: to the chicken stock add $1/2$ tsp salt, sugar, 1 tsp light soy sauce, oyster sauce, sesame oil and a good shake of pepper.

4. Heat 2 Tbsp cooking oil and brown ginger, shallot and garlic slices. Add mushrooms and chicken legs. Stir to mix. Add gravy mixture, cover the pan and allow to simmer for 30–40 minutes. When cooked, the mushrooms and chicken legs should be tender and the gravy thick. Season to taste.

5. Boil $1/2$ cup water in another pan. Add $1/4$ tsp salt and the cabbage leaves. Cover and cook for 2 minutes.

6. Arrange boiled cabbage leaves on a serving dish and mushrooms and chicken legs on top. Serve hot.

Note: For a variation of this dish, try adding sliced tinned abalone to the mushrooms and chicken legs just before serving. Use the abalone liquid as stock for gravy. Abalone should be cooked only long enough to heat it up. Over-cooking toughens it.

Almond Chicken

Preparation time 30 min • *Cooking time* 15 min • *Serves* 4–6

Almonds 1 cup
Chicken thigh 1, deboned
Chicken gizzards 4
Tapioca flour 3 tsp
Light soy sauce 1 tsp
Rice wine 2 tsp
Salt $^1/_2$ tsp
Water $1^1/_2$ cups
Water chestnuts 1 cup, diced
Cooking oil for deep-frying
Chinese mushrooms 4, soaked,
   cleaned and diced
Onions 2, diced
Sugar $^1/_4$ tsp
Sesame oil $^1/_2$ tsp
A shake of pepper
Angled loofah (*ketola*) 1, diced
Spring onions 2, chopped
Coriander leaves 1 sprig

1. Blanch almonds and dry them. Clean chicken thigh and gizzards and dice them into 1-cm cubes. Season chicken thigh meat with 2 tsp tapioca flour, $^1/_4$ tsp light soy sauce, 1 tsp rice wine and $^1/_4$ tsp salt.

2. Boil 1 cup water in a pan add the water chestnuts and bring it back to boil. Remove and drain well. Keep the water for cooking.

3. Heat 1 cup cooking oil and deep-fry almonds in slightly smoking oil until light brown. Remove and drain. Remove all but 2 Tbsp oil and fry the chicken thigh meat for 1 minute. Then add the gizzards, mushrooms, water chestnuts and onions with the remaining water and cook for 3–4 minutes.

4. Mix ingredients for gravy: to 3 Tbsp water, add the remaining tapioca flour, salt and rice wine, together with sugar, $^1/_2$ tsp light soy sauce, sesame oil and a good shake of pepper. Mix well.

5. When meat is cooked, add the angled loofah, toss to mix well, then add the gravy mixture. When the angled loofah is cooked, season to taste and serve garnished with browned almonds, spring onions and coriander leaves.

Paper-wrapped Chicken

Paper-wrapped Chicken

Preparation time 10–15 min • *Cooking time* 4–5 min • *Serves* 4

Chicken meat 2 cups, cut into
    small pieces
Ginger juice extracted from 1-cm
    knob ginger
Light soy sauce 1 tsp
Rice wine 2 tsp
Salt $1/4$ tsp
Sugar $1/2$ tsp
Cooking oil for deep-frying
Greaseproof paper 12 (15-cm
    square pieces)

1. Season chicken with ginger juice, light soy sauce, rice wine, salt, sugar and $1/2$ Tbsp cooking oil. Leave for 30 minutes.

2. Divide chicken into 12 portions and place on well greased greaseproof paper. Wrap firmly to form little packets. Tuck the loose end of the paper into the folds or staple to secure.

3. Heat the oil for deep-frying and fry the packets for 2–3 minutes until paper browns. Drain well and serve.

Chicken Boiled in Soy Sauce

Preparation time 10 min • *Cooking time* 40 min • *Serves* 6–8

Water 2 cups
Light soy sauce 2 Tbsp
Dark soy sauce $1/2$ Tbsp
Rock sugar 1 thumb-sized piece
Cinnamon stick 2.5-cm length
Star anise 2 segments
Chicken 1 (about 1.5 kg)
Cooking oil
Cucumber and tomato slices

1. In a tall, narrow saucepan, boil water with light and dark soy sauce, rock sugar, cinnamon stick and star anise.

2. Clean chicken and put it into the boiling mixture. Cover the pan and simmer for 15–20 minutes. Turn off the heat and allow chicken to finish cooking for another 20 minutes.

3. Remove chicken and rub some cooking oil all over. Cut into pieces and place on a serving dish lined with sliced cucumber. Garnish with tomato slices. If desired, boil stock until much reduced in quantity, cool and pour some over the chicken.

Chicken Baked in Salt

Preparation time 10–15 min • *Cooking time* 40–50 min • *Serves* 6–8

Chicken 1 (about 1.5 kg)
Ginger 2.5-cm knob
Salt 1 tsp
Five spice powder (*ng heong fun*) $1/4$ tsp
Rice wine 1 Tbsp
Light soy sauce 2 tsp
Greaseproof paper 2 sheets
Rock salt 9 kg

1. Clean chicken and cut off legs. Hang it up to dry. Pound ginger and mix it with salt, five spice powder and rice wine. Pour this mixture into the cavity of the chicken and rub the whole interior evenly with it. Leave the chicken to season for 1 hour. Brush skin with light soy sauce and wrap chicken with 2 sheets of greaseproof paper.

2. Put rock salt in a large and deep wok and fry it till it is very hot. Make a well in the center and embed chicken in the salt. When chicken is completely covered with salt, cover the wok and leave it over low heat for 15 minutes. Turn off the heat and allow the chicken to bake in hot salt for another 15 minutes. It should then be cooked.

3. Unwrap the chicken very carefully, lift it onto a chopping board and pour out the juice into a bowl. Cut the chicken into bite-sized pieces and arrange them on a serving dish. Pour the juice over the chicken and serve with chilli sauce.

Note: Choose the oldest large wok in your possession, for the rock salt will leave pits in the wok. Two enamel basins can be used if no large, old wok is available.

Spicy Fried Chicken

Preparation time 10 min • *Cooking time* 10–15 • *Serves* 6–8

Chicken 1 (about 1.5 kg), skinned
Curry powder 1^1/$_2$ Tbsp
Dark soy sauce 1 Tbsp
Salt 1 tsp
Sugar ^{1}/$_4$ tsp
Cooking oil 10 Tbsp
Ginger 1-cm knob, sliced
Garlic 2 cloves, sliced
Curry leaves 1 sprig
Green chillies 2, slit into 6 parts each
Onion (optional) 1, sliced

1. Cut chicken into four. Season with curry powder, dark soy sauce, salt and sugar. Leave to marinate for 1 hour.

2. Heat cooking oil and fry ginger, garlic, curry leaves and chillies. Add chicken pieces and fry till well-cooked and brown. If onion is used, add when chicken is almost done.

Crispy Fried Chicken

Preparation time 20 min • *Cooking time* 20 min • *Serves* 6–8

Chicken 1 (about 1.5 kg)
Spiced salt ^{3}/$_4$ Tbsp (refer to page 52)
Cinnamon stick 7.5-cm length
Star anise 6 segments
Water 3 cups
Honey 1 Tbsp
Lime 1, quartered
Cooking oil for deep-frying

1. Clean chicken and cut off legs. Dry chicken thoroughly. Rub the inside of the chicken with spiced salt. Put a 3-cm stick of cinnamon and 3 segments of star anise inside the chicken and close the opening with a toothpick.

2. Boil water with the remaining cinnamon stick and star anise for 5 minutes and remove spices. Add honey and lime wedges and let it boil. When water boils, hold the chicken over the boiling water and ladle it over the chicken until the skin tightens and looks shiny.

3. Hang chicken in a breezy, sunny spot for 5 hours or until completely dry. Alternatively, dry chicken in front of a fan.

4. Heat cooking oil and fry chicken for 8–10 minutes until golden brown. Cut into large pieces and serve with spiced salt, chilli sauce and sweet plum sauce (*suin mui cheong*).

Fried Spring Chicken

Preparation time 25–30 min • *Cooking time* 15–20 min • *Serves* 6

Carrot 1
Green, unripe papaya 2.5-cm slice
Salt 3 tsp
Sugar 3 tsp
Vinegar 2 Tbsp
Spring chickens 3 (each about 450 g)
Ginger 4-cm knob
Light soy sauce 2 Tbsp
Sherry 1 Tbsp
Honey 1 tsp
A shake of pepper
Oil for deep-frying
Cucumber 1, sliced
Tomato 1, sliced

1. Slice carrot and green papaya and mix 1 tsp salt with it. After 5 minutes wash away the salt and dry sliced carrot and papaya on a paper napkin. Put carrot and papaya in a bowl and mix in sugar and vinegar. Allow carrot and papaya to pickle for at least 3 hours.

2. Clean spring chickens, cut away legs and hang them up to dry. Pound ginger to extract ginger juice. Mix together ginger juice, light soy sauce, sherry, honey, pepper and the remaining salt. Rub this mixture all over the chickens. Allow chickens to season for at least 2 hours.

3. Heat cooking oil for deep-frying. When oil is hot, fry each chicken for about 5 minutes until they are golden brown and cooked. Cut each chicken in half and serve on a serving dish garnished with cucumber and tomato slices and pickled carrot and papaya. Serve this dish with sweet plum sauce (*suin mui cheong*) or chilli sauce.

Fried Spring Chicken

Chicken Fried with Dried Chillies

Chicken Fried with Dried Chillies

Preparation time 20–25 min • Cooking time 5 min • Serves 4–6

Chicken meat 1^1/$_2$ cups
Dried red chillies ^{1}/$_2$ cup
Ginger 1-cm knob
Light soy sauce 2 Tbsp
Tapioca flour 3 tsp
Worcestershire sauce 1 tsp
Water ^{1}/$_4$ cup
Sesame oil ^{1}/$_2$ tsp
Rice wine 2 tsp
Sugar 1 tsp
Cooking oil 3 Tbsp

1. Cut the chicken meat into bite-sized pieces. Remove stems and seeds from dried red chillies, wash them very quickly, cut them into 2.5-cm lengths and dry them in the sun until crisp. Pound ginger to extract ginger juice. Season chicken meat in a marinade of 1 Tbsp light soy sauce, 2 tsp tapioca flour and ginger juice for at least 30 minutes.

2. Mix gravy ingredients: to the water add the remaining tapioca flour and soy sauce, together with Worcestershire sauce, sesame oil, rice wine and sugar. Mix well.

3. Heat cooking oil and fry dried red chillies over low heat for ^{1}/$_2$ minute until the chillies are a dark, reddish-brown colour. Remove dried chillies and keep aside. Remove all the oil before adding seasoned chicken and fry till chicken pieces are cooked (about 3–4 minutes). Add the gravy mixture and fry until the gravy thickens. Mix in the dried chillies, season to taste and serve.

Fried Chicken Strips with Button Mushrooms

Preparation time 30–40 min • Cooking time 6–10 min • Serves 6–8

Chicken 1 (about 1.5 kg)
Tapioca flour 2 Tbsp
Salt 2 tsp
Sugar 1 tsp
Egg white 1, beaten
Sesame oil 2 tsp
A shake of pepper
Water 1^1/$_4$ cups
Oyster sauce 2 Tbsp
Light soy sauce 2 tsp
Dark soy sauce ^{1}/$_2$ tsp
Flowering cabbage (*choy sum*)
    or lettuce 150 g
Cooking oil for deep-frying
Ginger 2.5-cm knob, shredded
Garlic 2 cloves, chopped
Button mushrooms 1 cup, sliced
Rice wine 1 Tbsp

1. Clean and debone the chicken. Cut chicken meat into strips. Leave aside ^{1}/$_2$ tsp tapioca flour and blend the rest with 1 tsp salt, ^{1}/$_2$ tsp sugar, beaten egg white, 1 tsp sesame oil and a good shake of pepper. Knead this marinade well into the chicken meat and leave for 20 minutes.

2. Mix gravy ingredients: to ^{1}/$_4$ cup water, add ^{1}/$_2$ tsp salt, the remaining sugar, sesame oil and tapioca flour, together with oyster sauce, light soy sauce, dark soy sauce and a good shake of pepper.

3. Boil the remaining water in a frying pan. When water boils, add ^{1}/$_2$ Tbsp oil and ^{1}/$_2$ tsp salt. Add flowering cabbage to boiling water to lightly cook them. Drain vegetables and lay them on a serving dish.

4. Heat the oil for deep-frying. When oil is hot, put in the seasoned chicken meat. Stir with chopsticks to separate the strips and cook until chicken changes colour—it takes about 1 minute. Remove chicken meat and drain well.

5. Remove all the oil from the pan. Heat the oily pan and fry ginger and garlic until they brown. Add the button mushrooms and fried chicken, mix well together, then add the gravy mixture. Stir well until gravy thickens. Now add the rice wine and season to taste. To serve, place chicken strips on the boiled vegetables.

Five Spice Chicken

Preparation time 10–15 min • Cooking time 6–8 min • Serves 6–8

Chicken 1 (about 1.5 kg)
Ginger 2.5-cm knob
Shallots 4
Five spice powder (*ng heong fun*) $^1/_2$ tsp
Salt 1 tsp
Sugar $^1/_2$ tsp
Light soy sauce 1 Tbsp
Sesame oil $^1/_2$ tsp
Rice wine 1 Tbsp
Pepper $^1/_4$ tsp
Egg yolk 1
Cornflour 5 Tbsp
Cooking oil for deep-frying

1. Clean chicken and cut it into 24 pieces. Pound ginger and shallots. Season chicken pieces with pounded ingredients, five spice powder, salt, sugar, soy sauce, sesame oil, rice wine and pepper. Leave it in the marinade for 2 hours. Beat the egg yolk and mix it with the seasoned chicken pieces. Coat each piece in cornflour.

2. Heat cooking oil for deep-frying and fry chicken pieces for about 4–5 minutes until they are golden brown and cooked. Drain well and serve with spiced salt (refer to page 34).

Note: Chicken pieces can be prepared hours before they are required. Simply remove from the oil once they are lightly browned and fry once more in very hot oil for 1 minute just before serving. This is useful when entertaining, as chicken can then be served crisp and hot.

Fried Chicken in Oyster Sauce

Preparation time 20 min • Cooking time 30–40 • Serves 6–8

Chicken 1 (about 2 kg)
Light soy sauce 1 Tbsp
Dark soy sauce 1 tsp
Dried Chinese mushrooms 6, soaked
Carrot 1, small
Spring onion 1
Garlic 3 cloves
Ginger 1-cm knob
Water 3 cups
Salt 1 tsp
Sugar 1 tsp
Oyster sauce 1 Tbsp
Sesame oil 1 tsp
Rice wine $^1/_2$ Tbsp
A shake of pepper
Cooking oil for deep-frying
Tapioca flour 1 tsp, blended with
    1 Tbsp water

1. Clean chicken and cut off the legs. Mix light soy sauce with $^1/_2$ tsp dark soy sauce and rub this mixture all over the chicken, inside and outside.

2. Halve the mushrooms. Cut the carrot into 1-cm slices and the spring onion into 4-cm lengths. Chop the garlic and pound the ginger to extract juice.

3. Mix ingredients for gravy: to the water, add salt, sugar, oyster sauce, sesame oil, rice wine, ginger juice, pepper and the remaining dark soy sauce.

4. Heat cooking oil for deep-frying and fry the chicken (whole) until it is golden brown all over. Remove and drain.

5. Remove all but 2 Tbsp oil, brown the garlic, then fry mushrooms and carrot for 1 minute. Add the gravy mixture and fried chicken. Cover and simmer for about 30 minutes until chicken is tender. If necessary, add more water. Turn chicken every 10 minutes to ensure even cooking.

6. Remove chicken, mushrooms and carrot from pan. Reduce quantity of the gravy by quick boiling until about 1 cup remains. Add tapioca flour mixture to thicken the gravy. When gravy boils, turn off the heat. Keep the gravy hot until it is required.

7. Cut the chicken into pieces and arrange neatly on a serving plate. Place mushrooms, carrot and spring onion on the chicken pieces and pour the gravy over the chicken before serving.

Seafood

Fried Fish with Turmeric

Fried Fish with Turmeric

Preparation time 20 min • Cooking time 10–15 min • Serves 4–6

Spanish mackerel (*ikan tenggiri*)
   1 (about 600 g)
Fresh turmeric (*kunyit*) 2, 5-cm knob
Salt $1/3$ tsp
Cooking oil for frying

1. Cut the fish into 1-cm cutlets.

2. Pound turmeric till very fine. Season fish with salt and turmeric. Marinate for at least 30 minutes. Fry seasoned fish in hot cooking oil until brown on both sides.

Note: For a spicier dish, use 1 Tbsp curry powder in place of turmeric to season the fish.

   Chubb mackerel (*ikan kembung*) can also be used in place of Spanish mackerel (*ikan tenggiri*). Clean the fish and make diagonal slits on either side of the fish.

Ikan Masak Lemak

(Fish in Spicy Coconut Gravy)

Preparation time 20 min • Cooking time 30 min • Serves 4

Dried red chillies 8
Shallots 5
Ginger 2.5-cm knob
Dried shrimp paste (*belacan*)
   2.5 x 2.5 x 0.5-cm piece
Salt 1 tsp
Lemon grass (*serai*) 1 stalk
Coconut $1/2$, grated
Water 1 cup
White pomfret (*ikan bawal putih*)
   1 (about 450 g)
Kaffir lime leaves (*daun limau purut*)
   (optional) 5

1. Pound together chillies, shallots, ginger, dried shrimp paste and salt. Bruise lemon grass and finely shred kaffir lime leaves (optional). Extract $1/2$ cup thick coconut milk from grated coconut, then add 1 cup water to grated coconut and extract a full cup of milk.

2. Put the second extraction (1 cup) of coconut milk, pounded ingredients and bruised lemon grass into a pan and let it boil slowly till it is fairly thick. While gravy is boiling, scale the fish and remove entrails. Clean it and cut it into 4–5 pieces. Rub each piece very lightly with salt.

3. When gravy is thick enough, put fish into it and let it simmer till fish is cooked. Add the first extraction ($1/2$ cup) of coconut milk and shredded kaffir lime leaves (optional) and continue cooking until oil rises to the top. Season well before serving.

Note: Threadfin (*ikan kurau*) can be used in place of white pomfret.

Steamed Grouper

Preparation time 25–30 min • Cooking time 12 min • Serves 4–6

Grouper 1 (about 600 g)
Lean pork 50 g
Dried Chinese mushrooms 3, soaked
    to soften
Ginger 6 thin slices
Water 4 tsp
Cooking oil 1 Tbsp
Light soy sauce 1 tsp
Sesame oil 1 tsp
A few shakes of pepper
Spring onion 4 tsp, chopped
Coriander leaves 2 tsp, chopped

1. Clean grouper and cut pork into strips. Cut mushrooms into 0.25-cm thick slices. Shred the ginger slices very finely.

2. Mix gravy ingredients: to the water, add cooking oil, light soy sauce, sesame oil and pepper.

3. Place grouper on an enamel plate, arrange the mushrooms and pork neatly on the fish and spoon the gravy mixture over the whole fish. Steam fish over boiling water for 12 minutes.

4. Remove steamed fish from the steamer, transfer it to a clean and warmed serving plate quickly. Garnish fish with spring onion and coriander leaves. Serve at once.

Note: White pomfret (*bawal putih* or *bawal tambah*) can be used in place of grouper.

Sweet Sour Fish

Preparation time 30 min • Cooking time 10–15 min • Serves 4–6

Pomfret (*ikan bawal*) 1 (about 600 g)
Salt 1$^{1}/_{2}$ tsp
Sugar 2$^{1}/_{2}$ tsp
Egg white 1
Cornflour 6 Tbsp
Water 3 Tbsp + $^{1}/_{2}$ cup
Cucumber $^{1}/_{2}$
Chilli 1
Spring onions 5
Coriander leaves 5 sprigs
Garlic 2 cloves
Tomato sauce 4 Tbsp
Vinegar $^{1}/_{2}$ Tbsp
Cooking oil for deep-frying

1. Clean pomfret. Remove the head and slit it in half, taking care not to cut through the skin at the top of the head. Fillet the fish. Score the 2 pieces of fish lengthwise and crosswise without cutting through the skin.

2. In a big, flat plate, mix 1 tsp salt, $^{1}/_{2}$ tsp sugar, egg white, 3 Tbsp cornflour and 3 Tbsp water. Marinate the fillet and the fish head too, if preferred, in this mixture. Leave the fish in the marinade for 15–20 minutes.

3. Clean and shred cucumber, chilli and spring onions. Cut the coriander leaves into 2.5-cm lengths and chop the garlic finely. In a bowl, mix $^{1}/_{2}$ cup water, tomato sauce and vinegar, the remaining sugar and $^{1}/_{2}$ tsp salt together with 2 tsp cornflour.

4. Heat enough cooking oil for deep-frying. Dredge seasoned fish with the remaining cornflour and fry in hot oil until brown and crisp. Place fried fish on a warmed serving dish.

5. In a clean frying pan, heat 2 tsp cooking oil and brown the garlic. Add the tomato sauce mixture, stirring gently till gravy boils and thickens. Season this gravy well before pouring over the fried fish. Garnish fish by arranging shredded cucumber around it and sprinkling sliced chilli, spring onions and coriander leaves on top of it.

Acar Fish (Pickled Fish)

Preparation time 20 min • Cooking time 15 min • Serves 4–6

Spanish mackerel (*ikan tenggiri*)
   1 (about 600 g)
Salt 1 tsp
Shallots 8
Garlic 8 cloves
Fresh turmeric (*kunyit*) 7.5-cm knob
Chillies 2
Cooking oil 4 Tbsp
Vinegar ¹/₂ cup
Sugar 4 tsp

1. Slice fish into 1-cm cutlets. Wash them and drain, then rub a little salt into each cutlet. Peel shallots, garlic and turmeric. Slice them thinly and dry the slices in the sun for 2–3 hours. Remove seeds from chillies and shred very thinly. Dry well.

2. Heat cooking oil and fry fish cutlets till evenly browned on both sides. Lay them as flat as possible in an enamel bowl or earthenware jar.

3. Remove all but 1 Tbsp cooking oil from the frying pan and fry dry turmeric until oil is yellow in colour. Remove turmeric and add vinegar, salt and sugar. When vinegar comes to a boil, lower heat and taste it. Add more salt and sugar, if necessary.

4. Sprinkle shredded chillies and the dry shallot and garlic slices over the fish cutlets and pour vinegar mixture over it. Let fish soak in vinegar for at least 6 hours before serving. It is best to make it the day before serving.

Note: Pickled fish will keep very well in the refrigerator for up to a week.

Gulai Asam Pedas
(Spicy and Sour Fish Curry)
Preparation time 25 min • *Cooking time* 20 min • *Serves* 4–6

Wolf herring (*ikan parang*) 600-g piece
Salt 1 tsp
Red chillies 8
Shallots 15
Fresh turmeric (*kunyit*) 2.5-cm knob
Lemon grass (*serai*) 2 stalks
Dried shrimp paste (*belacan*)
  2.5 x 2.5 x 0.5-cm piece
Dried sour fruit (*asam gelugur*) 2 slices
Water 1 cup

1. Clean the fish and rub a little salt all over it. Pound together chillies, shallots, turmeric, lemon grass and dried shrimp paste.

2. Stir the pounded ingredients and the dried sour fruit in water in a pan and let it simmer for 5–10 minutes to blend the flavours.

3. Add the fish and 1/2 tsp salt and let it simmer for another 10 minutes or until fish is cooked. Season to taste by adding more salt, if necessary. A good pinch of sugar may be added, if preferred.

Note: Long beans, cut into 4-cm lengths, can be added to this curry if desired.

Gulai Tumis
(Fish Chilli Curry)
Preparation time 10 min • *Cooking time* 10 min • *Serves* 4–6

White pomfret (*ikan bawal putih*)
  1 (about 600 g)
Lemon grass (*serai*) 2 stalks
Shallots 12–15
Garlic 6 cloves
Red chillies 8–10
Fresh turmeric (*kunyit*) 2.5-cm knob
Dried shrimp paste (*belacan*)
  2.5 x 2.5 x 0.5-cm piece
Tamarind pulp 1 Tbsp
Cooking oil 2 Tbsp
Pineapple 1 cup, sliced wedges
Lady's fingers 12, small
Salt to taste

1. Clean the fish and cut it into 5 or 6 pieces. Clean and slice lemon grass. Pound it together with shallots, garlic, chillies, turmeric and dried shrimp paste. Prepare 1 cup tamarind juice from the tamarind pulp and strain it.

2. Heat cooking oil in an earthenware pot (*belanga*) and fry pounded ingredients for 2–3 minutes until the oil separates from the ingredients.

3. Add salt and tamarind juice and let it come to a boil. Add pineapple and let it simmer for 5 minutes. Add the fish and allow the fish to simmer for 5 minutes before adding the lady's fingers. Cook for another 2–3 minutes. Season to taste.

Note: Black pomfret (*ikan bawal hitam*) and threadfin (*ikan kurau*) can be used as substitutes to white pomfret in this recipe.

Otak-Otak

Preparation time 40–50 min • Cooking time 20 min • Serves 4

Dried red chillies 6
Shallots 6
Peppercorns (optional) 12
Lemon grass (*serai*) 1 stalk
Galangal (*lengkuas*) 1 slice
Dried shrimp paste (*belacan*)
　2.5 x 2.5 x 0.5-cm piece
Candlenuts (*buah keras*) 2
Garlic 1 clove
Fresh turmeric (*kunyit*) 1.5-cm knob
Coconut $^1/_2$, grated
Eggs 2
Kaffir lime leaves (*daun limau purut*) 5,
　finely shredded
Sugar $^1/_2$ tsp
Salt $^1/_2$ tsp
Banana leaves 6–8, 15–20-cm
　square pieces
Pointed pepper leaves (*daun kaduk*)
　6–8
Threadfin (*ikan kurau*) 300 g, cut into
　1-cm slices

1. Pound together dried chillies, shallots, peppercorns, lemon grass, galangal, dried shrimp paste, candlenuts, garlic and turmeric until fine. Add some water to the grated coconut and extract $^1/_2$ cup coconut milk. In a big bowl, beat the eggs with a wooden spoon and add the pounded ingredients, kaffir lime leaves, sugar, salt and coconut milk. Mix well.

2. Scald banana leaves to soften them. Wash and dry the leaves. On each leaf, place one piece of pointed pepper leaf and 2 slices of fish. Top with 3–4 dsp of egg mixture. Wrap neatly and fasten with a stapler. Repeat until ingredients are used up.

3. Steam the packets over boiling water for 15–20 minutes.

Note: Fish roe, fish paste, Spanish mackerel (*ikan tenggiri*) or sole (*ikan lidah*) can be substituted for threadfin (*ikan kurau*). Otak-Otak can be cooked in a heatproof dish. In this case, steam over slowly boiling water for about 1 hour for a smooth custard.

Fish Paste

(Basic Recipe)

Preparation time 20 min

Spanish mackerel (*ikan tenggiri*) 500 g
Water 1$^1/_3$ cups
Salt 1$^1/_4$ tsp

1. Clean fish and fillet it. With a tablespoon, scrape off all the flesh from bones and skin.

2. Put the fish meat into a food processor or cake mixer and beat on medium speed for 7–8 minutes, gradually adding in the water until the meat becomes a soft, smooth paste. Add salt and continue beating for another 8–10 minutes until the fish paste firms up and looks shiny.

Note: This fish paste can be used for any dish requiring fish paste, such as *Yong Towfoo* (page 71), Egg and Fish Roll (page 68) and Thai Fish Cake (page 67). This fish paste can also be shaped into patties and fried to be put in sandwiches and salads. Fried fish patties can be stored in the fridge for up to a week.

Steamed Bean Curd with Fish Paste

Preparation time 15 min • *Cooking time* 10 min • *Serves 5*

Soft bean curd roll 1, cut evenly into
    10 rounds
Fish paste $^1/_2$ cup (*refer to Fish Paste recipe*)
Red chilli 5 thin rings
Coriander leaves 5
Water $^1/_4$ cup
Oyster sauce 2 tsp
A pinch of sugar
Tapioca flour $^1/_2$ tsp
Cooking oil $^1/_2$ Tbsp
Garlic $^1/_2$ tsp, chopped
A shake of pepper
Spring onion 1, chopped

1. Place the rounds of bean curd on a metal plate and dry the top surface with kitchen muslin. Spread 1 tsp fish paste to cover each piece of bean curd evenly. Press a chilli ring into the top of 5 bean curd rounds and a coriander leaf on the other 5 bean curd rounds.

2. Steam the bean curd for 6–7 minutes to cook the fish paste. Transfer the bean curd onto a warm serving dish.

3. Pour the liquid from the steamed bean curd into a cup and add water to make up $^1/_2$ cup liquid. Add the oyster sauce, sugar and tapioca flour to it and mix well.

4. Heat up cooking oil in a frying pan, lightly brown the garlic and add the gravy mixture, stirring until it boils. Season to taste and pour the gravy over the bean curd.

5. Sprinkle a little pepper and serve garnished with spring onion.

Steamed Tilapia with Preserved Soy Bean

Preparation time 20 min • *Cooking time* 15 min • *Serves 4–5*

Cooking oil $^1/_2$ Tbsp
Garlic 1 clove, chopped
Ginger 3 slices, chopped
Preserved soy beans (*tow cheong*)
　　1 Tbsp, mashed
Sugar $^1/_4$ tsp
Water 2 Tbsp
Red chilli (optional) $^1/_2$, chopped
Tilapia 300–400 g, scaled and dressed
Spring onion 1, chopped
Coriander leaves 1 sprig, chopped

1. Heat cooking oil in a frying pan and lightly fry the garlic and ginger before adding in preserved soy bean paste and sugar. Add water, mix the gravy well until it begins to thicken. Remove from heat and add chopped chilli (optional).

2. Place fish in a heatproof serving dish, pour the gravy over it and steam over boiling water for 10–12 minutes. Test to see if fish is cooked. Push a small knife into the thickest part of the fish to see if the flesh will come away from the bone. If the flesh comes away easily, the fish is cooked.

3. Serve immediately, garnished with spring onion and coriander leaves.

Fried Stuffed Hardtail

Preparation time 20 min • *Cooking time* 20 min • *Serves* 4

Red chillies 2
Shallots 3
Dried prawns 1 Tbsp
Hardtail (*ikan cencaru*) 1,
   medium-sized, skinned
Salt 1 tsp
Cooking oil for frying
Sugar ¹/₄ tsp
Lime 1, cut into wedges

1. Pound together chillies and shallots till fine. Wash dried prawns and pound them separately. Clean the fish and make a slit on each side along the back fin. Rub salt all over the fish.

2. Heat 1 Tbsp cooking oil and fry pounded chillies and shallots 2–3 minutes before adding dried prawns and sugar. Fry all together until well mixed.

3. Wash the fish once more to remove excess salt and dry it. Stuff slits and the cavity of the fish with the fried ingredients.

4. Heat 4 Tbsp cooking oil and fry the fish in it until it is well cooked and brown on both sides. This takes about 5 minutes for each side. Serve fish with lime wedges.

Note: Stuffed hardtail can also be grilled. If grilling, do not skin it as the skin protects the fish and keeps it moist. When cooked, the skin can be easily removed.

Fish Cakes

Preparation time 30 min • *Cooking time* 10 min • *Serves* 6

Threadfin (*ikan kurau*) 300 g
Onion ¹/₂, diced
Cooking oil for deep-frying
Potatoes 300 g, boiled, skinned and
   mashed
Spring onions 2, chopped
Egg 1, large, yolk and white separated
Salt 1 tsp
A shake of pepper
Plain flour for dusting
Breadcrumbs 1 cup

1. Clean fish and steam over boiling water. When cooked, remove skin and bones and flake the flesh. Fry the diced onion in 3 tsp hot cooking oil until light brown.

2. Mix flaked fish, mashed potatoes, browned onion, spring onions, egg yolk, salt and pepper in a bowl. Taste and add more salt and pepper if necessary.

3. Flour a pastry board and shape a tablespoonful of mixture at a time into a round cake. Beat the egg white in a shallow plate. Spread breadcrumbs on a sheet of greaseproof paper or plastic.

4. Coat fish cakes with egg white and toss in the breadcrumbs. Deep-fry fish cakes until golden brown, drain and serve.

Tod Mon Pla

(Thai Fish Cake)

Preparation time 30 min • *Cooking time* 20 min • *Serves* 6

Lemon grass (*serai*) 2 stalks, ground
Galangal (*lengkuas*) 2 slices, ground
Kaffir lime leaves (*daun limau purut*) 5,
    finely shredded
Long beans 1 cup, finely sliced
Fish paste 300 g (*refer to page 16*)
Sugar $1/2$ tsp
Egg 1
Cooking oil 1 cup
Cucumber 6 slices
Tomato 6 slices

1. Mix all the ingredients except cooking oil, cucumber and tomato together quickly, stirring to mix thoroughly. Divide the mixture into 12 portions and shape each portion into a round pattie.

2. Heat up the cooking oil in a wok and fry the patties until golden brown on both sides. Drain fried patties on kitchen paper before arranging them on a serving dish.

3. Garnish with cucumber and tomato slices and serve with *cucumber sauce.

Note: Add 2 tsp of ground chillies to get a spicier fish cake if preferred. When spices are added to fish paste, cook as soon as possible as the spices will change the texture of the fish paste if cooking is delayed. For cocktails, use 1 tsp of the mixture for each pattie. This recipe makes about 50 cocktail patties.

*Cucumber Sauce

Cucumber 1 Tbsp, coarsely chopped
Red chillies 2, finely chopped
Vinegar 1 tsp
Sugar $1/2$ tsp
Fish sauce $1/4$ cup

1. Mix the ingredients and serve with Thai Fish Cake.

Egg and Fish Roll

Preparation time 45–50 min • Cooking time 30 min • Serves 6

Spanish mackerel (*ikan tenggiri*) 600 g
Tapioca flour 2 tsp
Salt 1$^1/_2$ tsp
A shake of pepper
Water about 5 Tbsp
Eggs 3
Cooking oil $^1/_4$ Tbsp

1. Clean fish and fillet it. With a tablespoon, scrape off all the flesh from bones and skin. Pound the flesh in a mortar until it becomes a smooth paste.

2. Return the paste to a big bowl and add tapioca flour, 1 tsp salt, a good shake of pepper and water. Stir ingredients together quickly to get a well blended tacky paste. If paste looks firm and thick, add more water to it. The paste should be soft and sticky.

3. Beat the eggs with $^1/_2$ tsp salt. Heat cooking oil in a frying pan and make 3 thin omelettes.

4. Spread the omelettes on a chopping board and spread a portion of fish paste on each omelette. Use a wet knife to prevent paste sticking to it. The paste should be evenly spread over the whole surface of the omelette. Roll up each omelette into a tight roll. Place the rolls in a steamer and steam over boiling water for 30 minutes.

5. Slice the Egg and Fish Roll into 0.5-cm slices and serve with chilli sauce.

Note: This recipe provides the traditional way in which to make fish paste. Refer to page 64 on how to make fish paste using a food processor or cake mixer.

Prawn Sambal

Preparation time 30 min • *Cooking time* 15 min • *Serves 4–6*

Prawns 300 g, medium-sized
Sugar 1/2 tsp
Salt 1 tsp
Red chillies 12
Shallots 12
Lemon grass (*serai*) 1 stalk
Candlenuts (*buah keras*) 3
Dried shrimp paste (*belacan*)
    2.5 x 2.5 x 0.5-cm piece
Tamarind pulp 1 Tbsp
Cooking oil 2 Tbsp
Tomatoes 4, quartered

1. Shell and devein prawns. Season with sugar and 1/2 tsp salt. Pound together chillies, shallots, lemon grass, candlenuts and dried shrimp paste. Prepare 1/2 cup tamarind juice from tamarind pulp. Strain it.

2. Heat cooking oil and fry pounded ingredients for 3–4 minutes. Add prawns and stir till prawns are lightly cooked. Add tomatoes and tamarind juice. Simmer till prawns are cooked, tomatoes are tender and gravy is beginning to thicken. Season to taste before serving.

Fried Tamarind Prawns

Preparation time 25 min • *Cooking time* 15–20 min • *Serves 6–8*

Prawns 600 g, large
Tamarind pulp 2 Tbsp
Salt 1 1/2 tsp
Sugar 1/2 tsp
Water 2 Tbsp
Cooking oil 5 Tbsp
Cucumber 1/2

1. Cut away feelers and sac from the head of the prawns and remove shell between the head and tail. Slit the back of the shelled portion and devein.

2. Mix tamarind with salt, sugar and water. Marinate prawns in this mixture for at least 1 hour.

3. Heat cooking oil and fry the prawns until they are dark brown on both sides. Serve garnished with cucumber slices.

Note: Black pomfret (*ikan bawal hitam*) or Spanish mackerel (*ikan tenggiri*) can be used in place of prawns in this recipe.

Prawn and Pineapple Curry

Preparation time 30 min • *Cooking time* 25–30 min • *Serves* 4–6

Pineapple $^1/_2$
Prawns 300 g, medium-sized
Salt $1^1/_2$ tsp
Coconut $^1/_2$, grated
Red chillies 10
Shallot 10
Candlenuts (*buah keras*) 5
Lemon grass (*serai*) 1 stalk
Galangal (*lengkuas*) 2.5-cm knob
Fresh turmeric (*kunyit*) 2.5-cm knob
Dried shrimp paste (*belacan*)
    2.5 x 2.5 x 0.5-cm piece
Cooking oil 2 Tbsp

1. Skin, quarter and cut off the hard central core of the pineapple. Slice each quarter into 1-cm wedge-shaped pieces. Shell, devein and season prawns with a little salt.

2. Extract $^1/_2$ cup first coconut milk and 1 cup second coconut milk from the grated coconut. Grind together chillies, shallots, candlenuts, lemon grass, galangal, turmeric and dried shrimp paste.

3. Heat cooking oil in a clay pot and fry the ground ingredients till the oil separates from the ingredients. Add the prawns and cook for another 2 minutes.

4. Add half of the second extraction of coconut milk to help cook the prawns thoroughly. Take out the prawns and set them aside. Add the rest of the second extraction of coconut milk and when it boils again, add the pineapple wedges and 1 tsp salt. Let it simmer slowly till pineapple is tender (about 15 minutes).

5. Return prawns to the curry and add the first extraction ($^1/_2$ cup) of coconut milk, stirring all the while until the curry boils again. Turn off heat immediately and season the curry before serving.

Fried Prawns with Garlic Salt

Preparation time 20 min • *Cooking time* 4–5 min • *Serves* 6–8

Prawns 600 g, medium-sized
Salt 1 tsp
Cooking oil 6 cups
Shallots 2, sliced
Garlic 6 cloves, chopped finely
Red chilli 1/2, chopped finely
Sherry or rice wine 2 Tbsp
A shake of pepper

1. Leave the prawns unshelled but cut away feelers and legs and remove the sac from the head. Wash in salt water to remove any sliminess from the shell, then drain and dry.

2. Heat cooking oil in a frying pan. When oil is smoking hot, fry the prawns until they are cooked (about 2 minutes). Remove prawns from oil and keep aside.

3. Pour out all the oil from the pan. In the same pan, coated with oil, fry shallots and garlic until light brown. Then add the chilli, salt and sherry, and finally the fried prawns. Toss all together and remove at once. Dust with a little pepper and serve immediately.

Note: A pinch of five spice powder (*ng heong fun*) can be added to this dish, if desired.

Yong Towfoo
(Stuffed Bean Curd)

Preparation time 1 hr • *Cooking time* 20 min • *Serves* 4–6

Spanish mackerel (*ikan tenggiri*) 300 g
Firm bean curd (*pak towfoo*) 10 pieces
Red chillies 4
Salt 1 1/2 tsp
Tapioca flour 1 tsp
Sugar 1/2 tsp
Light soy sauce 1 tsp
A shake of pepper
Water 3/4 cup
Cooking oil 4 Tbsp
Spring onions 4, cut into 2.5-cm lengths
Sesame oil 1 tsp (optional)

1. Clean the fish and make fish paste (*refer to page 64*).

2. Wash bean curd and cut each piece diagonally into 2 triangular pieces. Make a deep slit along the diagonal edge, leaving the other 2 edges intact. Slit chillies lengthwise and remove seeds. Stuff bean curd and chillies with fish paste, using a knife which is dipped into salt water frequently to prevent sticking and to give a smooth finish.

3. Prepare the gravy: mix 1/2 tsp tapioca flour, 1/2 tsp salt, the remaining sugar, 1 tsp light soy sauce and a good shake of pepper with 1/4 cup water.

4. Heat cooking oil and fry bean curd and chillies lightly with fish side in the oil. When the fish side is lightly brown, add the remaining water and cook gently for 15 minutes.

5. Mix the gravy well and add it to the bean curd together with the spring onions. Season well before serving. If preferred, add 1 tsp sesame oil. Serve with chilli sauce.

Note: Other vegetables like eggplant, lady's finger and bitter gourd can also be stuffed and served in this dish.

Seafood Tom Yam

Preparation time 30 min • *Cooking time* 45 min • *Serves* 4–5

Stock 1.5 litres
Galangal (*lengkuas*) 4 slices
Lemon grass (*serai*) 2 stalks, cut into 2.5-cm lengths
Kaffir lime leaves (*daun limau purut*) 5
Dried grass mushrooms (optional) 10, soaked and softened
Bird's eye chillies (*cili padi*) 8–10, cut into 0.5-cm slices
Button mushrooms 6–8, cut in half
Prawns 10–12, medium, shelled but leaving tails intact
Grouper or red snapper 150 g, cut into thick slices
Squid (*sotong*) 2, medium, score and cut into 5–6 pieces
Small lime (*limau kesturi*) juice 3–4 Tbsp
Fish sauce 1 Tbsp
Chinese celery 1 sprig, cut into 3-cm lengths

1. Boil stock with galangal, lemon grass, kaffir lime leaves, dried grass mushrooms and bird's eye chillies for 10 minutes to extract flavour from the spices. Boil until stock is reduced to 1 litre.

2. Add button mushrooms, prawns, fish and squid and continue boiling for 3–4 minutes. Add lime juice and fish sauce. Season to taste with salt and more lime juice, if necessary.

3. Serve garnished with Chinese celery.

Note: Tom Yam is delicious served with bean sprouts and vermicelli. To adapt this recipe to make Chicken Tom Yam, use 250 g chicken meat instead of seafood.

Mussels in Preserved Soy Bean Paste

Preparation time 20 min • *Cooking time* 10 min • *Serves 4–6*

Mussels 600 g
Garlic 3 clove
Shallots 3
Ginger 2.5-cm knob
Red chilli 1
Preserved soy beans (*tow cheong*)
   1 Tbsp
Cooking oil 1 Tbsp
Sugar 1 tsp

1. Put mussels in a colander and agitate colander under a running tap to get rid of all the sand. Take each mussel and try to slide the 2 halves of the shell across each other. If they slide, they will be filled with mud and should be discarded. Leave fresh mussels in a basin of water for at least 1 hour. Drain them and plunge them into a pot of boiling water. Leave for 1 minute. Drain well.

2. Chop the garlic and shallots. Shred ginger finely and cut chillies into 2-mm rings. Mash preserved soy beans.

3. Heat cooking oil in a wok and lightly brown garlic and shallots. Add preserved soy bean paste and stir gently for 3–4 minutes. Add ginger, chillies and mussels and stir-fry over high flame for a minute before adding sugar. Continue stir-frying till mussels are all split open, indicating that they are cooked. If necessary, reduce gravy a little. Season and serve hot.

Sambal Ikan Bilis

(Dried Anchovy Sambal)

Preparation time 20–25 min • *Cooking time* 10 min • *Serves* 4

Dried red chillies 8
Shallots 8
Candlenuts (*buah keras*) 3
Dried shrimp paste (*belacan*)
 2.5 x 2.5 x 0.5-cm piece
Tamarind pulp 1 Tbsp
Water $^1/_2$ cup
Dried anchovies (*ikan bilis*) $^3/_4$ cup,
 heads and entrails removed
Cooking oil $^1/_4$ cup
Salt $^1/_2$ tsp
Sugar 1 tsp

1. Pound together chillies, shallots, candlenuts and dried shrimp paste until fine. Squeeze tamarind in water to get juice. Wash dried anchovies briefly and drain dry.

2. Heat cooking oil and fry dried anchovies until crisp and brown. Drain and leave aside.

3. Fry pounded ingredients in the same oil for 2–3 minutes. Add tamarind juice, salt and sugar and cook it slowly till gravy is thick. Season to taste, add fried dried anchovies and remove from heat at once.

**Dried Anchovies
(*Ikan Bilis/Kong Yu Chai*)**

Although dried anchovies can be cooked whole, you may also remove the head and intestines. Then rinse quickly and dry thoroughly before using. Fry them in deep-fat and they make delicious crisp titbits for cocktails.

Bean Curd
and Eggs

Mah Poh Towfoo (Bean Curd in Chilli Sauce)

Mah Poh Towfoo

(Bean Curd in Chilli Sauce)

Preparation time 15 min • *Cooking time* 15–20 min • *Serves* 4–6

Soft bean curd (*towfoo*) 4 square pieces
Shallots 2
Garlic 2 cloves
Ginger 1-cm knob
Spring onions 2
Preserved soy beans (*tow cheong*)
    1 Tbsp
Stock $^1/_2$ cup
Light soy sauce 2 tsp
A shake of pepper
Cooking oil 2 Tbsp
Pork 1 cup, minced
Ground chilli 2 tsp
Rice wine 1 Tbsp
Tapioca flour 1 tsp, blended with
    1 Tbsp water

1. Cut bean curd into 2.5-cm cubes. Chop shallots, garlic and ginger. Chop spring onions and mash preserved soy beans.

2. Mix gravy ingredients: to the stock, add light soy sauce and pepper.

3. Heat cooking oil and fry shallots, garlic and ginger for 1 minute. When they begin to brown, add preserved soy bean paste and ground chilli. Fry for another minute before adding the pork. Stir well to separate pork and fry until it is cooked.

4. Add bean curd cubes to the meat mixture, then the rice wine. Mix carefully so as not to break the bean curd before adding the gravy mixture. Cook slowly for about 5 minutes. Slow cooking is necessary to keep bean curd tender. Thicken gravy with tapioca flour mixture. Season to taste. Add chopped spring onion before serving.

Note: Vary the amount of ground chilli to individual taste.

Bean Curd with Vegetables

Preparation time 20 min • *Cooking time* 6–7 min • *Serves* 4

Soft bean curd (*towfoo*) 7.5 x 15-cm piece
Lean pork 225 g
Carrot 1, medium-sized
Baby corn 6 cobs
Water chestnuts 6
Shallots 2
Garlic 2 cloves
Snow peas 1 cup
Water $^1/_2$ cup
Light soy sauce 2 tsp
Oyster sauce 1 tsp
Sesame oil $^1/_2$ tsp
Salt 1 tsp
Sugar $^1/_2$ tsp
A shake of pepper
Cooking oil 3 Tbsp
Tapioca flour 1 tsp, blended with
    1 tsp water
Rice wine 1 Tbsp

1. Wash the bean curd, place it in an ice tray and freeze it for at least 12 hours. Defrost it before it is required and press out the water. With the knife held at an angle of 45 degrees, slice the bean curd into 0.5-cm slices.

2. Clean and slice the pork, carrot, baby corn cobs and water chestnuts. Chop shallots and garlic. String the snow peas.

3. Mix gravy ingredients: in water, mix light soy sauce, oyster sauce, sesame oil, salt, sugar and pepper.

4. Heat 2 Tbsp cooking oil and fry snow peas until they are lightly cooked. Take out and keep aside.

5. Heat the remaining cooking oil, brown shallots and garlic and fry pork slices till the pieces separate. Add the bean curd, carrots, baby corns and water chestnuts and fry all together until well mixed. Add the gravy mixture, cover the pan and cook for 3–4 minutes. When vegetables are cooked, add the snow peas and thicken the gravy with tapioca flour mixture. Add the rice wine before seasoning to taste. Sprinkle with pepper before serving.

Note: Bean curd prepared this way has a very different texture that somewhat resembles tripe. Instead of pork, prawns may be used.

Sun Kong Towfoo
(Bean Curd with Crabmeat)

Preparation time 20 min • Cooking time 15–20 min • Serves 4–6

Soft bean curd (*towfoo*)
   15 x 10 x 5-cm piece
Lean pork $^1/_4$ cup
Carrot 1, small
Button mushrooms $^1/_2$ cup
Spring onions 2
Snow peas 15
Stock 1 cup
Salt 1 tsp
Fish sauce 2 tsp
Sugar $^1/_2$ tsp
Oyster sauce 1 tsp
Sesame oil $^1/_2$ tsp
A shake of pepper
Cooking oil for deep-frying
Ginger 3 slices
Crabmeat $^1/_4$ cup
Tapioca flour 1 tsp, blended with
   1 Tbsp water
Egg 1, beaten

1. Wash bean curd carefully and chill for at least 4 hours. Half lengthwise and cut each half into 6 equal slices just before cooking. Slice pork, carrot and button mushrooms. Cut spring onions into 4-cm lengths. String and wash snow peas.

2. Mix gravy ingredients: to the stock, add salt, fish sauce, sugar, oyster sauce, sesame oil and pepper. Mix well.

3. Heat cooking oil for deep-frying and fry cold bean curd pieces until brown on both sides. Remove bean curd pieces to a dish.

4. Leave 1 Tbsp cooking oil in pan. Fry snow peas, add salt. Fry till snow peas are bright green. Remove and place with bean curd pieces.

5. Heat 1 Tbsp cooking oil and fry ginger slices until lightly browned. Add pork, carrots and button mushrooms and toss together for another minute. Add gravy mixture and allow to boil for 1 minute before adding fried bean curd and snow peas. After another 2–3 minutes, add crabmeat. Thicken the gravy with tapioca flour mixture. Season to taste and turn off heat.

6. Add spring onions and beaten egg to the hot food, stir well and serve with a good shake of pepper.

Note: Use the type of bean curd that is made in a slab. The sides and edges are firmer and is easier to handle.

Egg Sambal

Preparation time 30 min • Cooking time 5–10 min • Serves 5

Eggs 5, hard-boiled, shelled and halved
Red chillies 12
Shallots 10
Dried shrimp paste (*belacan*)
   2.5 x 2.5 x 0.5-cm piece
Lemon grass (*serai*) 1 stalk
Coconut $^1/_2$, grated
Water 3 Tbsp
Tamarind pulp 1 Tbsp
Cooking oil 2 Tbsp
Salt 1 tsp

1. Arrange egg halves on dish, yolk side up. Grind chillies, shallots, dried shrimp paste and lemon grass together. Extract 1 cup coconut milk. Add water to tamarind and extract juice.

2. Make the *sambal*: heat cooking oil. Fry ground ingredients and salt for about 3 minutes. Add coconut milk and cook for 2–3 minutes before adding tamarind juice. Season to taste and pour *sambal* over eggs. Serve with cucumber slices and rice.

Scrambled Eggs with Crabmeat

Preparation time 10–15 min • Cooking time 5–8 min • Serves 4–6

Bamboo shoots $^1/_4$ cup, shredded
Eggs 5
Salt $1^1/_2$ tsp
Sesame oil 1 tsp
A shake of pepper
Cooking oil 3 Tbsp
Crabmeat $^1/_2$ cup
Spring onion 1, cut into 4-cm lengths
Bombay onion 1, cut into thin slices

1. Squeeze out water from bamboo shoots. Beat eggs with salt, sesame oil, pepper and 1 Tbsp cooking oil. Mix in crabmeat, bamboo shoots and spring onion.

2. Heat the remaining cooking oil and fry onion until limp. Add egg mixture and scramble until lightly cooked. Serve with pepper.

Note: For variety, scramble eggs with prawns and angled loofah (*ketola*), Chinese sausages and onions.

Egg Sambal

Bean Curd in Clay Pot

Preparation time 20 min • *Cooking time* 20–25 min • *Serves* 4–6

Soft bean curd (*towfoo*) 4 square pieces
Dried Chinese mushrooms 5, soaked to soften
Red chillies 2
Stock 1 cup
Light soy sauce 2 tsp
Dark soy sauce $1/2$ tsp
Oyster sauce 2 tsp
Sesame oil 1 tsp
Salt $1/2$ tsp
Sugar $1/4$ tsp
A shake of pepper
Cooking oil for deep-frying
Ginger 1-cm knob, sliced
Garlic 2 cloves, chopped
Preserved soy beans (*tow cheong*)
    1 Tbsp, mashed
Pork 125 g, sliced
Bamboo shoot $1/2$ cup, sliced
Carrot 1, small, sliced
Water 1 cup, mixed with $1/2$ Tbsp
cooking oil
Flowering cabbage (*choy sum*) 6 stalks,
    plucked to 5-cm lengths
Tapioca flour $1/2$ tsp, blended with
    2 tsp water

1. Wash and cut bean curd squares diagonally into 8 triangular pieces. Halve mushrooms. Remove seeds from chillies and cut each diagonally into 6–8 pieces.

2. Mix gravy ingredients: to the stock, add light and dark soy sauce, oyster sauce, sesame oil, salt, sugar and pepper.

3. Heat cooking oil for deep-frying and fry bean curd pieces until brown. Drain well and keep aside.

4. In a clay pot, heat 2 Tbsp cooking oil and brown ginger slices and garlic. Add preserved soy bean paste and fry for 2 minutes. Then add pork, bamboo shoot, mushrooms, carrot and chilli and fry together for another 2 minutes. Add the fried bean curd pieces and gravy mixture. Cover the pot and let the contents simmer for 10 minutes.

5. Boil water-and-oil mixture in a pan. Put in flowering cabbage, cover and cook for 1 minute until greens are cooked. Drain well.

6. Thicken gravy in the clay pot by adding the tapioca flour mixture. Season to taste and arrange flowering cabbage all round the top. Sprinkle with pepper and serve.

Kwai Fah Chee

(Shark's Fin with Eggs)

Preparation time 4 hr • *Cooking time* 10 min • *Serves* 4–6

Shark's fin 1 cup
Chicken stock 4 cups
Water chestnuts $1/4$ cup
Spring onion 1
Water 1 cup
Eggs 4
Crabmeat 1 cup
Salt 1 tsp
A pinch of ground cinnamon
A shake of pepper
Cooking oil $2 1/2$ Tbsp

1. Soak shark's fin in hot water until it is soft and loose. Drain, then boil in chicken stock for about 4 hours. Rinse in cold water, drain and remove bits of skin which may be found stuck to the shark's fin.

2. Peel and shred water chestnuts and cut spring onion into 4-cm lengths. Heat water in a pan and when it boils, add water chestnuts. As soon as water re-boils, turn off the heat and drain water chestnuts.

3. Beat the eggs and add shark's fin, crabmeat, water chestnuts and spring onion. Also add salt, cinnamon and pepper. Mix the ingredients well.

4. Heat 2 Tbsp cooking oil in a pan. When it is hot, pour in the mixed ingredients and scramble until it sets very lightly. Just when the mixture begins to set, add the remaining cooking oil and continue to scramble until it is completely set. Serve immediately with a good shake of pepper.

Note: If water chestnuts are not available, use bamboo shoots instead. *Kwai Fah Chee* is often served with lettuce leaves.

Vegetables

Stuffed Fried Bean Curd with Chilli and Plum Sauce

Stuffed Fried Bean Curd with Chilli and Plum Sauce

Preparation time 8 min • *Cooking time* 2 min • *Serves* 4

Lettuce 1 leaf, shredded
Fried soft bean curd (*chou towfoo*)
   4 pieces, blanched, drained and cut into
   2 rectangles each
Bean sprouts $1/2$ cup, tailed and blanched
Cucumber $1/2$ (about 6-cm long), shredded

1. Spread shredded lettuce on a serving dish. Set aside.

2. Slit the soft centre of each piece of bean curd to make a pocket.

3. Mix the bean sprouts and shredded cucumber and stuff it into the bean curd pocket.

4. Arrange stuffed bean curd neatly on the bed of shredded lettuce and serve with *chilli plum sauce.

*Chilli Plum Sauce

Red chillies 4, finely ground
Garlic 1 clove, finely ground
Lime juice 3–4 Tbsp
Sugar 1–2 tsp or to taste
Salt $1/2$ tsp or to taste
Plum sauce 2 Tbsp
Sesame seeds 1 tsp, roasted and
   lightly crushed
Peanuts 2 tsp, roasted and crushed

1. Mix the ground chillies, garlic, lime juice, sugar and salt in a bowl.

2. Stir in the plum sauce, sesame seeds and peanuts and serve with the stuffed bean curd.

Bean Curd Fried with Angled Loofah

Preparation time 8 min • *Cooking time* 5 min • *Serves* 5

Cooking oil 1 Tbsp
Garlic 1 clove, finely chopped
Fried soft bean curd (*chou towfoo*)
   3 pieces, quartered
Stock 1 cup
Angled loofah (*ketola*) 1, skinned, cut
   lengthwise and sliced into 2.5-cm pieces
Oyster sauce 2 tsp
Tapioca flour $1/2$ tsp, blended with 1 Tbsp
   water
Light soy sauce to taste
A shake of pepper

1. Heat cooking oil and lightly brown the garlic. Add bean curd and stock, and as soon as it boils, add the angled loofah and oyster sauce.

2. Lower the heat and stir the mixture gently for 1 minute, being careful not to break the bean curd.

3. Thicken the gravy with the tapioca flour mixture. Season with soy sauce and a shake of pepper. Serve immediately.

Note: Fried soft bean curd (*chou towfoo*) is brown on the outside, while the inside is smooth and soft. It is available in most markets.
   Fish paste (refer to page 64) shaped into 4-cm long fingers and steamed on a greased plate, can also be added to this dish.

Braised Vegetable Marrow

Preparation time 25 min • Cooking time 40 min • Serves 4–6

Vegetable marrow 1, large
Prawns $^1/_2$ cup, medium-sized
Sugar $^1/_2$ tsp
Salt 1 tsp
Dried Chinese mushrooms 5, soaked
    to soften
Lean pork $^1/_2$ cup
Water 1 cup
Fish sauce 1 Tbsp
A shake of pepper
Cooking oil for deep-frying
Shallots 2, sliced
Tapioca flour 1 tsp, blended with 1 Tbsp
    water
Spring onion 1, cut into 4-cm lengths
Red chilli 1, chopped

1. Scrape off the skin of the vegetable marrow. Cut the marrow in half down the length and cut each half diagonally into 2–3 pieces. Each piece should be about 7.5-cm long.

2. Shell and devein the prawns, and after cleaning, season with a pinch of each sugar and salt. Finely shred mushrooms and pork.

3. Mix gravy ingredients: in the water, mix the remaining sugar and salt, fish sauce and pepper.

4. Heat cooking oil for deep-frying. Fry the marrow pieces until brown all over. Set aside.

5. Remove all but 1 Tbsp cooking oil. Brown shallots, then fry pork, mushrooms and prawns until they change colour. Add fried vegetable marrow and the gravy mixture, cover and allow the marrow to simmer slowly until tender, about 30 minutes.

6. When the marrow is tender, boil quickly to reduce gravy if necessary and then thicken gravy with tapioca flour mixture. Season to taste.

7. To serve, arrange vegetable marrow pieces, rounded side upwards, on a serving dish and pour gravy over them. Garnish with cut spring onion and chopped chilli.

Stuffed Marrow

Preparation time 30–35 min • Cooking time 40 min • Serves 4–6

Vegetable marrow 1
Shrimps $^1/_4$ cup
Onion $^1/_2$
Pork or chicken $^1/_4$ cup, minced
Yam bean (*bangkuang*) 1 Tbsp,
    finely diced
Tapioca flour 1 tsp
Salt $^3/_4$ tsp
Sesame oil 1 tsp
A shake of pepper
Cooking oil 6 Tbsp
Water 1 cup
Tapioca flour mixture blended from
    $^1/_2$ tsp tapioca flour and 1 Tbsp water
Spring onion 1, chopped

1. Scrape off the skin of the vegetable marrow, clean it and scoop out the central pith with a teaspoon. Shell, clean and chop the shrimps. Dice the onion to get 1 tablespoonful. Mix chopped shrimps, minced meat, yam bean, onion, tapioca flour, $^1/_2$ tsp salt, sesame oil and a good shake of pepper. Knead the mixture to get the ingredients well-mixed and tacky. Stuff the vegetable marrow with this mixture.

2. Heat cooking oil in a saucepan large enough to hold the marrow and fry the marrow, turning it frequently until evenly browned. When marrow is evenly browned, remove all the oil from the pan. Add water with the remaining salt to the pan. Cover the pan and allow the vegetable marrow to simmer for 30 minutes until it is tender.

3. Thicken the gravy with tapioca flour mixture. Add the spring onion, season to taste and serve whole or sliced.

Stuffed Marrow

Fried Shredded Vegetable Marrow

Preparation time 15 min • *Cooking time* 10 min • *Serves* 4–6

Vegetable marrow 1
Transparent noodles (*fun see* or
  sohoon) 15 strands, soaked to soften
Dried prawns 1 Tbsp, soaked
Cooking oil 2 Tbsp
Shallots 2, sliced
Salt $^1/_2$ tsp
Water $^1/_4$ cup
Spring onion 1, cut into 4-cm lengths
Light soy sauce 1 tsp
A shake of pepper

1. Skin, clean and shred the vegetable marrow. Cut soaked transparent noodles into 5-cm lengths. Drain soaked dried prawns.

2. Heat cooking oil, brown sliced shallots and fry dried prawns for 1 minute. Add shredded vegetable marrow and salt and toss till well mixed. Add water, cover and cook for 5 minutes.

3. When the marrow is tender, add transparent noodles and spring onion and stir-fry until well mixed. Season with light soy sauce and serve with a good shake of pepper.

Note: Vegetable marrow may be substituted with cucumber or chocho in this recipe.

Chinese White Cabbage with Crab and Egg Sauce

Preparation time 30–35 min • *Cooking time* 40 min • *Serves* 4–6

Chinese cabbage 600 g
Stock 1 cup
Evaporated milk 2 Tbsp
Salt 1 tsp
Sugar $^1/_2$ tsp
Sesame oil $^1/_2$ tsp
A shake of pepper
Water 2 cups
Cooking oil 2 Tbsp
Fish sauce 2 tsp
Shallots 2, sliced
Crabmeat $^1/_2$ cup
Tapioca flour 1 tsp, blended with
  1 Tbsp water
Egg 1, beaten

1. Discard any old cabbage leaves and use only the tender young leaves at the centre of the Chinese cabbage. Wash and cut into 5-cm lengths. Drain.

2. Mix gravy ingredients: to the stock, add evaporated milk, $^1/_2$ tsp salt, sugar, sesame oil and pepper.

3. Boil water with $^1/_4$ tsp salt in a pan and when it boils, put in the white cabbage. Cover and cook for 5 minutes. Rinse vegetables in cold water to stop further cooking and drain well.

4. Heat 1 Tbsp cooking oil in a pan and toss cabbage in this. Add fish sauce. Arrange cabbage leaves on a serving dish.

5. Heat the remaining cooking oil and brown the shallots. Add the gravy mixture and when gravy boils, add the crabmeat. Thicken the gravy with tapioca flour mixture. Season to taste and turn off the heat. Add beaten egg, stir once and pour this gravy over the cabbage. Sprinkle pepper on top and serve at once.

Eggplant with Crab Sauce

Preparation time 10 min • *Cooking time* 25 min • *Serves 4–6*

Eggplants 5
Water 1 cup
Fish sauce 1 Tbsp
Vinegar 1 Tbsp
Sugar 1 tsp
Cooking oil 2 Tbsp
Garlic 2 cloves, chopped
Crabmeat $^1/_2$ cup
Tapioca flour $^1/_2$ tsp, blended with
    1 Tbsp water
A shake of pepper
Red chilli 1, shredded

1. Grill the eggplants until they are soft and cooked. Skin them and cut them into halves lengthwise and cut each length into quarters. Lay the pieces on a serving dish.

2. Mix gravy ingredients: in the water, mix fish sauce, vinegar and sugar.

3. Heat cooking oil and brown the garlic. Add the gravy mixture and then the crabmeat. When the gravy boils, thicken it with tapioca flour mixture. Season gravy to taste and pour over the eggplant. Sprinkle a good shake of pepper over the gravy and garnish with shredded chilli before serving.

Note: Eggplants can be boiled instead of grilled, if desired.

Gado-Gado (Vegetables with Peanut Sauce)

Gado-Gado
(Vegetables with Peanut Sauce)
Preparation time 40 min • *Cooking time* 20 min • *Serves* 4–6

Cooking oil for deep-frying
Firm bean curd (*pak towfoo*) 2 pieces
Water 1 cup
Salt $^1/_2$ tsp
Cabbage leaves 6, cut into 2-cm strips
Long beans 5, cut into 2.5-cm lengths
Bean sprouts 1 cup, tailed
Potato 1, boiled and sliced
Egg 1, boiled and sliced
Cucumber $^1/_2$, shredded

1. Heat cooking oil and fry the bean curd until the sides are lightly browned. Remove, drain and cool. Cut bean curd squares into 10–12 pieces.

2. Boil water with salt. Cook cabbage, long beans and scald bean sprouts. Drain well.

3. Arrange vegetables neatly on a serving dish with potato slices and garnish with egg slices and bean curd squares. Serve with *peanut sauce.

*Peanut Sauce

Red chillies 10
Shallots 8
Garlic 2 cloves
Dried shrimp paste (*belacan*)
   2.5 x 2.5 x 0.5-cm piece
Peanuts 1 cup, roasted
Tamarind pulp 1 Tbsp
Cooking oil 2 Tbsp
Palm sugar (*gula melaka*) 2 Tbsp,
   ground
Coconut milk 1 cup
Salt 1 tsp

1. Pound together chillies, shallots, garlic and dried shrimp paste until fine. Crush peanuts. Prepare $^1/_4$ cup tamarind juice from the tamarind pulp.

2. Heat cooking oil and fry pounded ingredients until well cooked. Add palm sugar, coconut milk and salt. Cook for 3–4 minutes before adding tamarind juice. When gravy is cooked and well blended, add crushed peanuts, season and serve with prepared vegetables.

Fried Eggplant
Preparation time 10 min • *Cooking time* 10 min • *Serves* 4–6

Eggplants 2
Salt 2 tsp, finely pounded
Peppercorns 10, finely pounded
Cooking oil 6–8 Tbsp

1. Slice eggplants diagonally into 1-cm thick slices and score the sides of each slice lightly. Mix salt and pepper and rub into the scored surfaces. Leave to season for 10–15 minutes.

2. Heat cooking oil and fry eggplant slices until evenly browned on both sides and cooked. Serve neatly arranged on a flat dish.

Loh Hon Chye
(Mixed Vegetables)
Preparation time 15 min • *Cooking time* 15–20 min • *Serves* 4–6

Dried Chinese mushrooms 6, soaked
   to soften
Cooking oil 2 Tbsp
Shallots 2, sliced
Mustard cabbage (*kai choy*) 1 head,
   cut into 2.5-cm lengths
Carrot 1, sliced
Salt 1 tsp
Water $^1/_2$ cup
Button mushrooms $^1/_2$ cup
Straw mushrooms $^1/_4$ cup
Fried gluten balls (*min kun*) 12
Tapioca flour $^1/_2$ tsp, blended with
   1 Tbsp water

1. Cut the Chinese mushrooms into halves.

2. Heat cooking oil, brown sliced shallots and fry mustard cabbage for 1 minute. Add carrot and Chinese mushrooms and toss all together till well mixed. Add salt and water. Cover the pan and allow vegetables to simmer for 10 minutes.

3. When vegetables are tender, add button and straw mushrooms and fried gluten balls. Cook for another 3–4 minutes. Thicken gravy with tapioca flour mixture. Season to taste and serve.

Fried Diced Long Beans

Preparation time 20–25 min • *Cooking time* 10 min • *Serves* 4–6

Preserved radish (*choy poh*) 1 Tbsp
Long beans 12 of green variety
Firm bean curd (*pak towfoo*) 1 piece
Prawns $1/2$ cup, medium-sized, shelled
Cooking oil 2 Tbsp
Shallots 2, sliced
Light soy sauce 1 tsp
Salt $1/2$ tsp
Water about 2 Tbsp
Peanuts 2 Tbsp, roasted
Chilli 1, finely chopped
A shake of pepper

1. Dice preserved radish into 0.5-cm cubes and soak in water. Dice the long beans, bean curd and prawns.

2. Heat cooking oil and fry the bean curd till lightly browned. Remove to a dish.

3. In the same cooking oil, brown the shallots, then add the prawns and stir-fry till they are cooked. Add preserved radish and long beans and toss all together. Combine light soy sauce, salt and water and pour this into the pan. Stir-fry for a few minutes until long beans are cooked. Finally, add the bean curd, peanuts and chilli, and toss to mix well. Season to taste and serve with a good shake of pepper.

Kerabu Kobis

(Cabbage Salad)

Preparation time 30 min • *Cooking time* 10–15 min • *Serves* 4–6

Dried shrimp paste (*belacan*)
    2.5 x 2.5 x 0.5-cm piece
Red chillies 3
Cabbage 300 g
Prawns 300 g, small
Coconut $1/2$, grated
Water 1 cup
Salt $1^1/2$ tsp
Shallots 6, sliced
Limes 3

1. Roast dried shrimp paste and pound with chillies to get *sambal belacan* (dried shrimp paste). Cut cabbage into 1-cm strips. Shell, devein and dice prawns. Using muslin cloth, extract coconut cream from the grated coconut.

2. Boil water with $1/2$ tsp salt. Put in cabbage. Remove cabbage as soon as water boils again. Drain well.

3. Put coconut cream to boil and allow it to simmer slowly until it begins to thicken. Add prawns and cook until it thickens again. Stir the mixture occasionally to prevent burning.

4. Halve limes, squeeze lime juice over sliced shallots and work in the *sambal belacan*. Add boiled cabbage and 1 tsp salt. Mix well together. Stir in coconut gravy, season to taste and serve.

Masak Lodeh
(Vegetables in Coconut Gravy)
Preparation time 20–25 min • *Cooking time* 10–15 min • *Serves* 4

Coconut 1, grated
Cooking oil 1 Tbsp
Garlic 2 cloves, sliced
Shallots 6, sliced
Prawns 1/4 cup, shelled and deveined
Galangal (*lengkuas*) 2 slices
Salt 1 tsp, or to taste
Red chillies 4, sliced
Cabbage 120 g, cut into 2-cm strips
Long beans 120 g, cut into 4 cm lengths
Eggplants 4, cut into 4-cm pieces and quarter
Soy bean cake (*tempeh*) 2 pieces,
   cut into 1-cm pieces

1. Extract 2 cups coconut milk from the grated coconut.

2. Heat cooking oil in a pan over medium heat and fry garlic and shallots for 1 minute. Add prawns and galangal, fry for another minute, then add coconut milk and salt. When coconut milk boils, add chillies, vegetables and soy bean cake pieces. Cover and allow coconut milk to come to a boil again.

3. As soon as coconut milk boils, remove the cover, stir continuously and cook for a further 4–5 minutes or until vegetables are tender. Season to taste and serve with Lontong (refer to page 17).

Acar Awak

(Vegetable Pickle with Sesame and Peanuts)

Preparation time 30 min • *Cooking time* 25 min

Cucumber 2, seeded and cut into
  3-cm fingers
Carrot 2, cut into 3-cm fingers
Water 3 cups
Vinegar 3 1/2 cups
French beans 10, cut into 3-cm lengths
Long beans 5, cut into 3-cm lengths
Red chillies 2, halved lengthwise and cut
  into 3 each
Cabbage 6 leaves, cut into 3 x 4-cm pieces
Cooking oil 1/2 cup
Sugar 4–5 Tbsp or to taste
Salt 2–3 tsp or to taste
Peanuts 1 cup, roasted, skinned and crushed
Sesame seeds 2 Tbsp, roasted

GRIND TOGETHER FINELY
Dried red chillies 15–20, soaked until soft
Fresh turmeric (*kunyit*) 1.5-cm knob
Lemon grass (*serai*) 2 stalks, thinly sliced
Galangal (*lengkuas*) 3 slices
Candlenuts (*buah keras*) 3
Shallots 20
Garlic 2 cloves
Dried shrimp paste (*belacan*) 3 x 3 x 0.5-cm piece

1. Place cucumber and carrot fingers in a colander, mix in
2 tsp salt and leave for 2–3 hours.

2. Boil water with 1 cup vinegar and 1 tsp salt in a saucepan.
Blanch French beans, long beans, red chillies and cabbage.
Drain blanched vegetables well before spreading them on
clean muslin to dry for at least 1 hour.

3. Shake the cucumber and carrot fingers well and spread to
dry on clean muslin.

4. Heat up the cooking oil in a wok and fry the ground
ingredients for 10–15 minutes. Add in the remaining vinegar,
sugar and salt to taste, and the crushed peanuts to get a thick
sauce. If necessary, fry a little longer to thicken the sauce. Turn
off the heat and mix in the air-dried vegetables. Lastly add in
the sesame seeds.

5. Cool Acar Awak before filling into sterilised bottles. Acar
Awak keeps well for up to 2 weeks in the fridge.

Acar Timun

(Cucumber Pickle)

Preparation time 1 hr • Cooking time 20–25 min

Cucumbers 2, cut into 2.5-cm fingers
Carrot 1, cut into 2.5-cm fingers
Red chilli 1, cut into 0.5-cm strips
Bombay onion 1, cut into 0.5-cm wedges
Salt 2 Tbsp
Dried red chillies 8
Shallots 8
Garlic 4 cloves
Ginger 2-cm knob
Candlenuts (*buah keras*) 3
Dried prawns $1/2$ cup
Cooking oil $1/2$ cup
Mustard seeds $1/2$ tsp
Turmeric powder $1/2$ tsp
Vinegar $3/4$ cup
Sugar $3 1/2$ Tbsp

1. Combine cut cucumbers, carrot, red chilli and onion and sprinkle with salt. Leave for at least 2 hours. When vegetables are limp, wash away salt and spread them out on a dry tea towel in a breezy place to dry.

2. Grind together dried red chillies, shallots, garlic, ginger and candlenuts. Pound dried prawns.

3. Heat cooking oil and fry mustard seeds for $1/2$ minute before adding ground ingredients and turmeric powder. Fry for another 3–4 minutes. When the ground ingredients separate from the oil, add dried prawns and continue cooking for another 2–3 minutes before adding vinegar and sugar. Cook slowly until the mixture is fairly thick. Season with more sugar and salt if necessary.

4. Stir in the prepared vegetables and toss quickly to mix well. Remove from heat. Cool before filling into warm bottles.

Note: It is best to leave the Acar Timun for 1 day before serving, for the flavours to be absorbed. Acar Timun keeps very well for a week or more.

Chinese Pickle

Preparation time 30 min

Cucumber 1
Chinese radish (*lopak*) 1, small
Carrot 1
Unripe papaya 1 slice
Red chillies 2
Salt 1 Tbsp
Vinegar 1 cup
Sugar 2–3 Tbsp

1. Clean and cut all vegetables into very thin slices. Sprinkle salt over them, toss to mix and leave for $1/2$ hour.

2. Wash vegetables to remove salt and press out all the water with a clean, dry tea towel. Leave them on a piece of muslin and allow them to dry in a breezy place for 1 hour.

3. When they are dry, place all vegetables in a bowl and add vinegar and sugar. Pour in enough vinegar to cover the vegetables. Season pickle to taste, adding more sugar if necessary. Leave pickle for at least 6 hours before serving.

Note: This pickle will keep, without refrigeration, in a cool place for up to a week. You may prepare pickled ginger, which is eaten with century eggs, using this recipe.

Kerabu Timun (Cucumber and Dried Prawn Salad)

Kerabu Timun
(Cucumber and Dried Prawn Salad)

Preparation time 20 min • *Cooking time* 6-8 min

Cucumbers 2
Dried prawns 1 Tbsp
Dried shrimp paste (*belacan*)
  2.5 x 2.5 x 0.5-cm piece
Red chillies 3
Shallots 6, sliced
Limes 3
Salt $^1/_2$ tsp
Sugar $^1/_2$ tsp

1. Skin and quarter the cucumbers. Cut away the soft centre and slice each quarter. Wash dried prawns and pound them.

2. Grill dried shrimp paste until it is brown on both sides. Pound chillies and grilled dried shrimp paste together to make *sambal belacan*.

3. Place sliced shallots in a large bowl and squeeze lime juice over them. Add the *sambal belacan* then the dried prawns, sliced cucumber, salt and sugar. Toss together to mix well, season to taste and serve.

Note: Substitute the cucumbers with pineapple for a sweet sour salad.

Fried Bean Sprouts with Prawns

Preparation time 30 min • *Cooking time* 5–7 min • *Serves* 4–6

Prawns 200 g
Sugar $^1/_2$ tsp
Salt 1 tsp
Water 4 Tbsp
Tapioca flour $^1/_2$ tsp
Light soy sauce 1 tsp
A shake of pepper
Cooking oil 1$^1/_2$ Tbsp
Firm bean curd (*pak towfoo*) 1 piece,
  cut into strips
Shallots 2, sliced
Bean sprouts 300 g, tailed
Spring onion 1, cut into 4-cm lengths
Chilli 1, shredded

1. Shell the prawns and slit them down the back. Devein, then wash and season with $^1/_4$ tsp sugar and $^1/_2$ tsp salt.

2. Mix gravy ingredients: to 3 Tbsp water, add tapioca flour, light soy sauce, the remaining sugar and salt and a good shake of pepper. Mix well.

3. Heat cooking oil and fry bean curd till firm. Remove to a dish. Brown the sliced shallots and fry prawns in the same oil for 1 minute. Add bean sprouts, bean curd, spring onion, chilli and the remaining water. Stir-fry for $^1/_2$ minute. Add the gravy mixture. When it thickens, season to taste and serve at once.

Note: Do not cover the pan when cooking bean sprouts as this may overcook the bean sprouts. Well-cooked bean sprouts should be firm and crisp.

Vegetarian Spring Rolls

Preparation time 1 hr • *Cooking time* 30 min • *Serves* 6–8

Cooking oil 1 cup
Hard bean curd (*teem chok*) 2 pieces,
    cut into thin strips
Shallots 2, sliced thinly
Yam bean (*bangkuang*) 1, medium,
    skinned and shredded
Carrot 1, shredded
Dried Chinese mushrooms 2–3, soaked
    and shredded
Salt $^1/_2$ tsp
French beans 8–10, shredded
Light soy sauce to taste
Dried bean curd sheet (*fu pei*) 1, divided
    into 16 square pieces, each 15-cm wide
Tapioca flour 2 tsp, blended with 1 Tbsp
    water into a paste
Water 1 cup
Vegetarian oyster sauce 2 tsp
Sugar $^1/_2$ tsp
Coriander leaves 1 sprig

1. Heat 2 Tbsp cooking oil and fry sweet bean curd strips until light brown. Drain and set aside.

2. Brown shallots, add yam bean, carrots and mushrooms. Mix well with salt and cook for 10 minutes. If it starts to burn, lower the heat, add about $^1/_4$ cup water and cook until the vegetables are a little soft but still crispy. Add the french beans and fried bean curd strips. Season to taste with soy sauce.

3. Spread the cooked vegetables on a large plate to cool. When cool, divide into 16 portions. This is the filling of the spring rolls.

4. Put one portion of vegetable filling on each piece of bean curd sheet in a diagonal position. Start folding and rolling from a corner to get a tight roll. Fold the two ends towards each other, spread a little tapioca flour paste along the sides of the last corner and roll over to complete making the roll. Repeat the process until all 16 rolls are made.

5. Heat 2 Tbsp cooking oil in a wok and fry the rolls, sealed side first, until lightly and evenly browned. Remove, drain and set aside. When all the rolls are browned, wipe the wok of excess oil before adding 1 cup water, oyster sauce, sugar and returning the rolls to the wok to simmer for 10 minutes. Season to taste and serve garnished with coriander leaves.

Pecal

(Boiled Vegetable Salad with Peanut Sauce)

Preparation time 1 hr • *Cooking time* 20 min • *Serves* 4–6

Sweet potato greens 200 g
Spinach 200 g, plucked to 4.5-cm lengths
Long beans 5, plucked to 4.5-cm lengths
Cabbage leaves 6, cut into 3 x 6-cm pieces
Salt 1 tsp
Dried chillies 15
Shallots 8–10
Tamarind pulp 1 level Tbsp
Plain flour 2 Tbsp
Water about 8 Tbsp
Peanuts 1 cup, roasted
Cooking oil 1 cup
Dried shrimp paste (*belacan*)
    2.5 x 2.5 x 0.5-cm piece
Palm sugar (*gula melaka*) 5 Tbsp

1. Peel fibrous skin from the stems of the sweet potato greens. Boil vegetables with a little salt until cooked. Drain well and set aside. Clean chillies and shallots, dry thoroughly. Remove seeds from the tamarind and press pulp into a cake.

2. Mix plain flour with water to get a thin batter. (Add the water a little at a time until the consistency is about right). Mix in $^1/_2$ cup roasted peanuts.

3. Heat cooking oil in a pan. When hot, ladle out peanut and batter mixture one tablespoon at a time and gently drop at the edge of the hot oil so that it forms a thin wafer. Fry till wafers are brown and crisp. Remove and drain well.

4. Using the same oil, fry dried chillies for about 15 seconds until lightly browned. Remove and fry shallots until cooked. Dish out shallots and fry tamarind for about 1 minute. Remove all but 1 Tbsp oil and fry dried shrimp paste until cooked. Lastly, toss the remaining roasted peanuts in the oily pan until peanuts are coated with oil.

5. Pound together fried chillies, shallots, dried shrimp paste, tamarind and peanuts until fine. Add palm sugar and salt.

6. To make Pecal gravy, mix pounded ingredients with a little boiled water. Serve gravy with boiled vegetables and crispy peanut wafers.

Note: This Pecal gravy can keep refrigerated for months. When required, mix as much as desired with a little warm water and serve with any variety of leafy vegetable. The amount of water added depends on the desired consistency.

Pecal (Boiled Vegetable Salad with Peanut Sauce)

Bitter Gourd Kerabu

Bitter Gourd Kerabu

Preparation time 20 min • *Serves* 5–6

Bitter gourd 1, cut lengthwise, seeds
   removed and thinly sliced
Walnuts 1 Tbsp, chopped
Raisins 2 Tbsp
Red chilli 1, shredded
Small limes (*limau kesturi*) 4–5,
   juice extracted
Sugar $1/2$ tsp
Salt $1^1/2$ tsp

1. Sprinkle 1 tsp salt over sliced bitter gourd, toss together
to mix evenly, and leave it aside for 20 minutes. The bitter
gourd slices should become limp. Wash the limp slices and
press out as much water as possible.

2. Put the bitter gourd in a bowl, add the walnuts, raisins,
chilli, lime juice and $1/2$ tsp sugar and mix together
thoroughly. Season to taste, adding more salt, sugar or
lime juice if necessary.

3. Chill in the fridge until ready to serve.

Lady's Fingers Fried with Prawns and Sambal

Preparation time 20 min • *Cooking time* 10 min • *Serves* 4

Red chillies 3
Bird's eye chillies (*cili padi*)
   (optional) 2
Shallots 5
Dried shrimp paste (*belacan*)
   1.5 x 1.5 x 0.5-cm piece
Cooking oil $1^1/2$ Tbsp
Prawns 100 g, small, shelled and deveined
Lady's fingers 250 g, diagonally sliced
   into 0.3-cm thick slices
Salt to taste
Water 6–8 Tbsp

1. Grind red chillies, bird's eye chillies (optional), shallots and
dried shrimp paste together. Heat cooking oil and fry ground
ingredients for 2–3 minutes.

2. Add the prawns and fry for another 2 minutes before adding
the lady's fingers. Mix well together and cook for a minute
before adding salt to taste. Add 3 Tbsp water, cover and leave
to cook for 2–3 minutes.

3. After 2–3 minutes, stir to prevent burning and to mix evenly.
If the mixture is too dry, add another 2–3 Tbsp water and
cover again to cook for another 2–3 minutes.

4. The lady's fingers should be just soft and not mushy when
ready. Season to taste and serve.

Daun Keledek Masak Lemak
(Sweet Potato Greens in Coconut Milk Gravy)
Preparation time 30 min • *Cooking time* 10 min • *Serves* 4–6

Sweet potato greens 500 g
Sweet potato 1
Red chillies 2
Shallots 4
Dried shrimp paste (*belacan*)
   2.5 x 2.5 x 0.5-cm piece
Coconut $^1/_2$, grated
Cooking oil 2 Tbsp
Dried prawns 1 Tbsp, soaked
   and drained
Salt 1 tsp

1. Clean sweet potato greens, peel tough fibrous skin from the stems and cut into 6.5-cm lengths. Peel and cut up sweet potato into 2.5-cm cubes. Pound together chillies, shallots and dried shrimp paste. Extract $^1/_4$ cup first coconut milk and 1 cup second coconut milk from the grated coconut.

2. Heat cooking oil and fry pounded ingredients for 2–3 minutes till the oil separates from the ingredients. Add the dried prawns and stir-fry for 1 minute before adding salt and the second extraction (1 cup) of coconut milk.

3. When the mixture boils, add sweet potato cubes. Cover and cook for 4–5 minutes. When the sweet potato is cooked, add the greens and the first extraction ($^1/_4$ cup) of coconut milk. As soon as it boils again, remove from heat. Season to taste and serve.

Note: Spinach, cabbage, *sayur manis* or *cekur manis**
and shredded chocho may be substituted for sweet potato greens.

*There is no English name for *sayur manis* or *cekur manis*, but the tender variety of this vegetable is often called 'Sabah vegetables' in Singapore and Malaysia.

Sambal Kelapa
(Spicy Dried Grated Coconut)
Preparation time 10 min • *Cooking time* 10–15 min

Red chilli $^1/_2$
Shallots 3
Galangal (*lengkuas*) 1 thin slice
Salt $^1/_2$ tsp
Cooking oil 1 Tbsp
Coconut 6 Tbsp, grated

1. Pound together chilli, shallots, galangal and salt.

2. Heat cooking oil in a pan over medium heat and fry pounded ingredients for 1–2 minutes. Add grated coconut and fry all together, stirring constantly until the coconut is dry and light brown.

3. Cool and store in a dry bottle till required.

Sambal Kangkung
(Water Convolvulus Fried with Sambal)
Preparation time 15 min • *Cooking time* 5 min • *Serves* 4

Red chillies 2
Bird's eye chillies (*cili padi*)
   (optional) 2
Dried shrimp paste (*belacan*)
   1.5 x 1.5 x 0.5-cm piece
Shallots 3
Cooking oil 1 Tbsp
Dried prawns 1 Tbsp, pounded
Water convolvulus (*kangkung*) 500 g,
   each leaf plucked with a 4–5-cm stem
Salt to taste

1. Pound the red chillies, bird's eye chillies (optional), dried shrimp paste and shallots together to make *sambal*.

2. Heat cooking oil and fry the pounded dried prawns with the *sambal* for 2 minutes.

3. Add the water convolvulus and a pinch of salt and fry quickly over a high flame.

4. The vegetable is cooked as soon as it looks limp. Season to taste and serve immediately.

Soups

Watercress and Pork Soup

Watercress and Pork Soup

Preparation time 15 min • Cooking time 1¹/₂ hr • Serves 4–6

Pork shoulder 300 g
Watercress 600 g
Water 8 cups
Light soy sauce 1 tsp
Salt 1 tsp
A shake of pepper

1. Clean the piece of pork, cutting away excess fat. Clean watercress and pluck off all green leaves and young shoots, leaving only the stems.

2. Place the piece of pork in a saucepan with water and bring it to a boil. Then add watercress stems (usually bound together with a piece of clean thread for easy removal later) and allow soup to simmer for 1–1¹/₂ hours.

3. When the soup is ready, take out the piece of pork and slice it into 0.5-cm thick slices. Remove watercress stems and throw them away. Bring soup to the boil again and add salt, watercress shoots and leaves. As soon as the soup boils again, remove it from heat and season to taste.

4. Take out watercress shoots and leaves and lay them on a serving dish. Arrange sliced pork on top and sprinkle light soy sauce and pepper over it before serving. Serve soup separately.

Note: If desired, add 2 preserved duck gizzards to the soup and boil them with the pork. As the gizzards are salty, taste before adding salt to the soup.

Steamed Melon Soup

Preparation time 30–35 min • Cooking time 1¹/₂ hr • Serves 4–6

Chinese winter melon 1 (about 3 kg)
Lotus seeds 3 Tbsp
Chicken meat 1 cup, diced
Dried Chinese mushrooms 4, soaked
    and diced
Button mushrooms ¹/₂ cup
Ginger 1-cm knob, sliced
Chicken stock 5 cups
Salt 2 tsp

1. Slice a piece about 2.5-cm thick from the top of the melon. With a tablespoon, scoop out the soft centre of the melon so that a melon bowl is obtained. The hollow should have a capacity of about 8 cups. The top of the melon bowl could be decorated by making serrated cuts around the edge.

2. Place the melon bowl in a large pan of boiling water, enough to cover the melon completely. Cover and cook over low heat for 20 minutes. Remove the melon and plunge it into a basin of cold water to cool. Drain well and stand melon bowl firmly in a heatproof bowl.

3. Soak the lotus seeds in cold water overnight to soften. Boil them for ¹/₂ hour until tender. Leave in cold water to cool, then peel off the skin, and with the help of a toothpick, push out the shoot from the top. These are tedious but necessary tasks as the brown skin would discolour the soup and the embryo is dreadfully bitter.

4. Place chicken meat, Chinese and button mushrooms, lotus seeds and ginger in the melon and add enough stock to fill slightly more than three quarters of the melon. Add salt and steam the melon for 1¹/₂ hours. Season to taste and serve hot.

Chicken and Corn Soup

Preparation time 15 min • *Cooking time* 8–10 min • *Serves* 4–6

Chicken meat 150 g, minced
Egg white 1
Water 3 Tbsp
Chicken stock 3 cups
Creamed corn 1 can
Salt 2 tsp
Light soy sauce 1 tsp
Sesame oil 1 tsp
A shake of pepper
Cooking oil 1 Tbsp
Cornflour 2 Tbsp, blended with
  3 Tbsp water

1. Mix chicken meat well with egg white and water.

2. Pour chicken stock into a large bowl and stir in creamed corn. Add salt, light soy sauce, sesame oil and pepper to season the mixture.

3. In a saucepan, heat cooking oil and pour in the seasoned corn mixture. Allow the mixture to boil for about 3 minutes. Thicken the soup by adding cornflour mixture, stirring all the while to prevent lumps forming. When soup is thick and boiling, stir in chicken meat. Remove soup from heat as soon as it boils again. Season and serve with a good shake of pepper.

Note: If desired, crabmeat may be added to this soup.

Szechuan Vegetable and Pork Soup

Preparation time 20 min • *Cooking time* 15 min • *Serves* 4–6

Lean pork 150 g, thinly sliced
Tapioca flour 1 tsp
Light soy sauce 1 tsp
A shake of pepper
Water 4 cups
Szechuan vegetable (*char choy*)
  $^1/_2$ cup, sliced
Sesame oil $^1/_2$ tsp
Spring onion 1, cut into 4-cm lengths

1. Season pork with tapioca flour, light soy sauce and pepper.

2. Heat water in a saucepan. When it boils, add Szechuan vegetable slices and allow to boil for about 4 minutes. Add sliced pork, stirring to separate the slices. After 2–3 minutes, add sesame oil and turn off heat. Season to taste. Add spring onion and serve with a good shake of pepper.

Pork, Liver and Chinese Spinach Soup

Preparation time 20 min • *Cooking time* 10 min • *Serves* 4–6

Lean pork 150 g, thinly sliced
Tapioca flour 1 tsp
Light soy sauce 1$^1/_2$ tsp
A shake of pepper
Pig's liver 90 g, thinly sliced
Ginger 2 slices, juice extracted
Salt $^1/_2$ tsp
Cooking oil 1 Tbsp
Shallots 2, sliced
Water 4 cups
Chinese spinach (*tong hoe*) 250–300 g

1. Season pork with $^1/_2$ tsp tapioca flour, $^1/_2$ tsp light soy sauce and a shake of pepper. Season liver with the remaining tapioca flour, ginger juice and $^1/_4$ tsp salt.

2. Heat cooking oil and brown shallots. Add water, the remaining light soy sauce and salt. When water boils, add pork slices, stirring to separate them. Cover and cook for 3 minutes. Add spinach and liver when the soup boils again. Remove from heat, season to taste and serve with a good shake of pepper.

Szechuan Vegetable and Pork Soup

Sweet Sour Soup

Sweet Sour Soup

Preparation time 45 min • Cooking time 20 min • Serves 4–6

Wood ear fungus (*mok yee*) 3 pieces,
  soaked
Lean pork 100 g
Ham or bacon 1 slice (ham) or 2 rashers
  (bacon)
Soft bean curd (*towfoo*) 1 piece
Dried Chinese mushrooms 3, soaked
Spring onions 2
Ginger 1-cm knob
Cornflour 1 tsp
Light soy sauce 1$^1/_2$ tsp
A good shake of pepper
Vinegar 2 Tbsp
Sesame oil 1 tsp
Stock 4 cups
Salt $^1/_2$ tsp
Sugar $^1/_2$ tsp
Cornflour mixture blended from
  1$^2/_3$ Tbsp cornflour and 3 Tbsp water
Egg 1, beaten

1. Clean and shred wood ear fungus. Shred the pork, ham or bacon, bean curd, mushrooms, spring onions and ginger.

2. Marinate pork in a mixture of 1 tsp cornflour, $^1/_2$ tsp light soy sauce and a shake of pepper. Mix the remaining light soy sauce, vinegar and sesame oil, a good shake of pepper and the shredded spring onions and ginger in a large soup bowl.

3. Place stock, salt and sugar in a saucepan and bring it to a boil. When the soup boils, add wood ear fungus, bean curd, mushrooms, ham or bacon and allow to boil for 2 minutes. Add the seasoned pork, stirring to separate the shreds. When the soup boils again, thicken it by adding the cornflour mixture. As soon as the soup boils again, turn off the heat.

4. Add egg slowly to the hot soup, stirring gently. Pour the soup over the seasoning in the soup bowl. Stir gently to mix, season to taste and serve hot.

Pork Balls and Bean Curd Soup

Preparation time 45 min • Cooking time 20 min • Serves 4–6

Pork shoulder 225 g, minced
Prawns $^1/_2$ cup, shelled and minced
Tapioca flour 1 tsp
Salt 1 tsp
Sesame oil $^1/_2$ tsp
A shake of pepper
Egg white 1, lightly beaten
Soft bean curd (*towfoo*) 2 pieces
Chinese cabbage 4 leaves
Cooking oil 1 Tbsp
Garlic 3 cloves, chopped
Shallots 2, sliced
Water 4 cups
Light soy sauce 1 tsp
Fish sauce 1 tsp

1. Mix together pork, prawns, tapioca flour, salt, sesame oil, a good shake of pepper and the egg white. Knead to mix well. Shape mixture into balls.

2. Cut the bean curd into 2.5-cm cubes. Cut the Chinese cabbage into 2.5-cm wide pieces.

3. Heat cooking oil in a saucepan and brown the garlic. Remove browned garlic to a small dish.

4. Brown shallots and add water combined with light soy sauce and fish sauce. When the water boils, add meatballs and allow them to cook for 2–3 minutes. When meatballs are cooked, add Chinese cabbage and bean curd. Allow the soup to simmer for another 3 minutes before turning off the heat and seasoning to taste. Serve the soup sprinkled with browned garlic.

Note: If desired, preserved cabbage (*tong choy*) can be added to this soup.

Beef and Radish Soup

Preparation time 10 min • *Cooking time* 1$\frac{1}{2}$ hr • *Serves* 4

Chinese radish (*lopak*) 1
Beef flank 300 g, cut into 4-cm cubes
Peppercorns 10
Star anise 1 segment
Water 6 cups
Salt 1 tsp
Light soy sauce 1 Tbsp
A shake of pepper
Spring onion 1, chopped

1. Halve the radish lengthwise and cut each half diagonally into 2.5-cm pieces.

2. Put beef, radish, peppercorns and star anise with water into a saucepan and let it come to a boil. When soup boils, lower heat and allow to simmer for at least 1$\frac{1}{2}$ hours.

3. When the soup is ready, it should have about 4 cups water. Season with salt, light soy sauce and pepper and serve garnished with spring onion.

Beef Soup

Preparation time 15–20 min • *Cooking time* 8–10 min • *Serves* 4

Beef steak 300 g, thinly sliced
Tapioca flour 1 tsp
Light soy sauce 2 tsp
Salt $\frac{3}{4}$ tsp
A shake of pepper
Soft bean curd (*towfoo*) 2 pieces
Cooking oil 2 Tbsp
Shallots 2, sliced
Water 3 cups
Green peas 2 Tbsp
Spring onion 1, chopped

1. Season beef slices with tapioca flour, soy sauce, $\frac{1}{4}$ tsp salt and pepper for at least 20 minutes. Clean and cut each piece of bean curd into 8–10 pieces.

2. Heat cooking oil in a saucepan and brown the shallots. Add water to browned shallots. When it comes to a boil, add the remaining salt, bean curd and green peas and allow to boil for 3 minutes. When peas are cooked, add the steak, stirring to separate the slices. As soon as the soup boils again, add chopped spring onion and remove from heat at once. Season to taste and serve with a good shake of pepper.

Note: As a quick one-dish meal, serve this soup with some rice vermicelli (*mee hoon*) or transparent noodles (*fun see* or *sohoon*). Soak the noodles in cold water to soften. Add rice vermicelli or transparent noodles with the steak. If desired, Chinese white cabbage or flowering cabbage (*choy sum*) may be used as a substitute for green peas.

Beef Soup

Sui Kow Soup

Sui Kow Soup

Preparation time 40 min • Cooking time 15 min • Serves 4

FILLING

Chicken meat $1/2$ cup, minced
Tapioca flour 1 tsp
Light soy sauce to taste
Prawns $1/2$ cup, small, shelled and coarsely chopped
Fish paste 2 Tbsp (*refer to page 111*)
Crabmeat (optional) 2 Tbsp
Carrot 1 Tbsp, finely chopped
Water chestnuts 1 Tbsp, chopped
Bombay onion 1 Tbsp, finely diced
Egg 1, beaten
Salt and pepper to taste
Spring onion 1 Tbsp, cut into 0.5-cm lengths

SOUP AND *SUI KOW*

Sui kow **skin** 24 pieces
Water 1.5 litres
Flowering cabbage (*choy sum*) 8–10 stalks, plucked into 5-cm lengths
Sesame oil $1/2$ tsp
Stock 1 litre

1. Place chicken meat, tapioca flour and $1/2$ tsp soy sauce in a bowl and knead together for 2 minutes. Add all the other filling ingredients to the chicken meat mixture and mix well together. Season this filling to taste.

2. Make the *sui kow*: place 1 tsp filling on each piece of *sui kow* skin. Lightly wet half the edge of the skin, fold the skin over the filling and press to seal the edges together.

3. Boil water in a saucepan. Put the flowering cabbage in. As soon as the water comes to the boil again, the vegetable is cooked. Drain the flowering cabbage well and place them in a serving bowl.

4. Bring the water to the boil again, put in half the quantity of *sui kow*. Leave for 5–7 minutes, making sure the filling is cooked. Drain them well and put them on top of the flowering cabbage.

5. When all the *sui kow* are cooked, sprinkle sesame oil over them. Heat up the stock, season to taste and pour it over the *sui kow*. Serve immediately with chilli sauce.

Wonton Soup

(Dumpling Soup)

Preparation time 30 min • Cooking time 10 min • Serves 4–6

Prawns 150 g, small
Sugar $1/2$ tsp
Salt $1/2$ tsp
Ginger 1-cm knob
Pork $1/4$ cup, minced
A shake of pepper
Wonton skins 25–30
Stock 4 cups
Fish sauce 2 tsp
Water 4 cups
Flowering cabbage (*choy sum*) 150 g, plucked to 5-cm lengths
Sesame oil $1/2$ tsp
Spring onions 2, chopped

1. Shell and devein prawns. Season with sugar and $1/4$ tsp salt for about 20 minutes, then rinse under a running tap and drain well. Chop the prawns coarsely.

2. Cut off 2 thin slices of ginger and pound the rest to extract ginger juice.

3. Season chopped prawns and minced pork with remaining salt, ginger juice and a good shake of pepper. Spread out each wonton skin and place a teaspoonful of the filling in the centre. Fold wonton skin over diagonally so that the opposite corners meet. Make another fold just below the filling to enable the folded corners to be drawn together. Press to seal the folded corners together with some water.

4. In a saucepan, boil stock, ginger slices, fish sauce and a good shake of pepper. Season soup to taste.

5. In another saucepan, boil water and add wonton and flowering cabbage. Cover and cook for 2 minutes. When a wonton is cooked, it floats. Drain cooked wonton and flowering cabbage and place in a serving bowl. Sprinkle sesame oil over the wontons and pour boiling soup over them. Garnish with chopped spring onion and a good shake of pepper and serve immediately.

Fish Ball Soup

Preparation time 30 min • *Cooking time* 40 min • *Serves 4–6*

FISH PASTE
Spanish mackerel (*ikan tenggiri*) 300 g
Water 4–5 Tbsp
Salt 2 1/2 tsp
Tapioca flour 1 tsp

SOUP
Preserved cabbage (*tong choy*) 1 tsp
Cooking oil 2 Tbsp
Garlic 2 cloves, chopped
Ginger 0.5-cm knob, sliced
Water 6 cups
Salt 1/2 tsp
Flowering cabbage (*choy sum*) 150 g,
    plucked to 5-cm lengths
Transparent noodles (*fun see* or *sohoon*)
    10 strands, soaked
Light soy sauce 1 Tbsp
A shake of pepper

FISH PASTE

1. Clean fish and fillet it. With a tablespoon, scrap off all the flesh from bones and skin. Keep fish bones and skin aside.

2. Put the fish meat into a food processor or cake mixer and beat on medium speed for 7–8 minutes, gradually adding in the water until the meat becomes a soft, smooth paste. Add 1 tsp salt and tapioca flour and continue beating for another 8–10 minutes until fish paste firms up and looks shiny.

3. Wet hands in salt water and shape fish paste into balls. Dip each fish ball in salt water before placing it on a plate to prevent them from sticking together.

SOUP

1. Wash preserved cabbage.

2. Heat cooking oil in a saucepan and brown the garlic. Remove browned garlic to a small dish.

3. Lightly brown the ginger slices in the hot oil and fry the reserved fish bones and skin for about 2 minutes before adding water and salt. Simmer for at least 30 minutes to get a good fish stock.

4. Strain the fish stock, return it to the saucepan and allow it to come to a boil before adding fish balls. When the soup boils again and fish balls are floating, add flowering cabbage, transparent noodles and preserved cabbage.

5. As soon as it boils, remove from heat, season it well with soy sauce, salt and pepper. Top with browned garlic and serve.

ABC Soup

Preparation time 20 min • *Cooking time* 30 min • *Serves 4–5*

Stock 1.5 litres
Chicken meat 1 cup, diced into
    1-cm pieces
White peppercorns 8, crushed lightly
Pumpkin (optional) 1 cup, skinned and
    diced into 1.5-cm cubes
Carrot 1 cup, skinned and diced into
    1.5-cm cubes
Potato 1 cup, skinned and diced into
    1.5-cm cubes
Bombay onion 1, diced
Celery (optional) 1 stick, diced
Salt to taste
Spring onion 1, chopped
Coriander leaves 1 sprig, chopped

1. Put stock, chicken meat and peppercorns in a large saucepan and bring to the boil. Lower heat and simmer for 10 minutes.

2. Add all the diced vegetables and bring it to the boil again. When it boils, turn the heat down and simmer for another 20 minutes.

3. Season with salt to taste and serve garnished with spring onion and coriander leaves.

Note: For a quick nourishing meal, boil 2 Tbsp macaroni in salt water for 10 minutes. Drain well and add to the soup before serving.

Noodles

Laksa Asam (Rice Vermicelli in Spicy and Sour Gravy)

Laksa Asam

(Rice Vermicelli in Spicy and Sour Gravy)

Preparation time 40–45 min • Cooking time 20–25 • Serves 4–5

Chubb mackerel (*ikan kembung*) 600 g
Water 6 cups
Red chillies 15
Shallots 15
Lemon grass (*serai*) 2 stalks
Dried shrimp paste (*belacan*)
    2.5 x 2.5 x 0.5-cm piece
Thick rice vermicelli 400 g
Tamarind pulp 1 heaped Tbsp
Polygonum leaves (*daun kesum*)
    a handful
Salt $1^1/_2$ tsp
Cucumber $^1/_2$, shredded
Pineapple 1 slice, shredded
Torch ginger bud (*bunga kantan*) 1,
    shredded
Onion 1, halved finely sliced
Mint leaves 1 cup, plucked from stalk
Limes 2, cut into wedges
Shrimp sauce (*petis* or *hay koh*) 1 Tbsp,
    mixed with 2 Tbsp water

1. Clean and boil fish in water until cooked. Take fish out, remove bones and flake flesh. Grind together 13 chillies, shallots, lemon grass and dried shrimp paste. Shred the remaining chillies. Soak rice vermicelli for about 30 minutes. Extract 2 cups tamarind juice from tamarind pulp and strain.

2. Add ground ingredients, tamarind juice, polygonum leaves and salt to fish stock and let simmer for 10–15 minutes. Season to taste and return flaked fish to gravy.

3. Boil rice vermicelli for 10–15 minutes until softened. Drain well.

4. Put equal portions of rice vermicelli in 6 serving bowls and pour boiling gravy over. Arrange prepared cucumber, pineapple, torch ginger, onion, chilli, mint leaves and limes on top of rice vermicelli or on a separate flat dish. Serve with shrimp sauce mixture in a separate bowl.

Laksa Lemak

(Rice Vermicelli in Spicy Coconut Gravy)

Preparation time 1 hr • Cooking time 30 min • Serves 4–5

Herring (*ikan parang*) or mackerel
    (*ikan kembung* or *ikan tenggiri*) 900 g
Thick rice vermicelli 400 g
Coconut $^1/_2$, grated
Lemon grass (*serai*) 1 stalk
Shallots 10
Peppercorns 6
Dried shrimp paste (*belacan*)
    2.5 x 2.5 x 0.5-cm piece
Cooking oil 3 Tbsp
Curry powder $1^1/_2$ Tbsp
Kaffir lime leaves (*daun limau purut*)
    (optional) 5, shredded
Salt $1^1/_2$ tsp
Cucumber $^1/_2$, shredded
Pineapple 1 slice, shredded
Red chilli 1, shredded
Limes 2, cut into wedges
Mint leaves 1 cup, plucked from stalk

1. Clean fish. Soak rice vermicelli for 30 minutes before boiling. Extract $^1/_2$ cup first coconut milk and 4 cups second coconut milk from grated coconut. Grind lemon grass, shallots, peppercorns and dried shrimp paste together.

2. Heat cooking oil. Fry ground ingredients and curry powder for about 5 minutes. Add second extraction (4 cups) of coconut milk and salt. When it boils, add cleaned fish. Allow fish to cook slowly for 10 minutes. When cooked, take it out, remove bones and flake flesh. Return flaked fish and add kaffir lime leaves (optional) to gravy and cook for another 2 minutes. Add first extraction ($^1/_2$ cup) of coconut milk and when it boils, turn off heat at once. Season to taste.

3. Drain soaked rice vermicelli and put into boiling water for 15 minutes or until soft. Drain well.

4. Arrange cucumber, pineapple and chilli shreds, lime wedges and mint leaves on a plate. Put equal portions of rice vermicelli into 6 serving bowls and pour gravy over it.

Note: To make Curry Mee with this recipe, use 600 g cockles, 225 g medium-sized prawns and $^1/_4$ chicken cut into small pieces instead of fish. Also add 4 squares of fried bean curd. The more common fine vermicelli, thick yellow noodles or even spaghetti may be used in place of thick rice vermicelli.

Mee Siam

(Fried Rice Vermicelli in Tangy Sauce)

Preparation time 25 min • *Cooking time* 20–25 min • *Serves* 4–6

Dried red chillies 8, soaked to soften
Shallots 15
Firm white bean curd (*pak towfoo*)
   2 pieces
Prawns 300 g, medium-sized
Rice vermicelli 225 g
Cooking oil $^1/_2$ cup
Garlic 2 cloves, chopped
Preserved soy beans (*tow cheong*)
   2 Tbsp, mashed
Water 1 cup
Sugar 1 Tbsp
Salt 1 tsp
Bean sprouts 2 cups, tailed
Chives (*kucai*) 6 stalks, cut into 5-cm
   lengths
Light soy sauce about 1 Tbsp
Red chillies 2, shredded
Egg 1, hard-boiled, shelled and sliced
Lime 2, cut into wedges

1. Pound softened dried chillies with 10 shallots. Slice the remaining shallots. Cut bean curd pieces into 2.5 x 0.5-cm pieces. Shell, devein and dice the prawns. Soak rice vermicelli in water to soften.

2. Heat 2 Tbsp cooking oil and fry bean curd slices until firm and lightly browned. Remove and drain well. Brown sliced shallots and keep them for garnishing. Brown garlic and fry preserved soy bean paste for 1 minute, then add water and sugar to it and let it simmer gently for 5–10 minutes to get a well flavoured gravy. Season to taste and serve in a sauceboat.

3. Heat the remaining cooking oil and fry the pounded ingredients for 1 minute. Add prawns, fried bean curd and $^1/_2$ tsp salt. Cook for 3–4 minutes until prawns are done. Dish up about half of this mixture for garnishing.

4. Add soaked rice vermicelli to the remaining mixture in the pan and toss until well mixed. Add bean sprouts, chives and light soy sauce. Toss together for another 2 minutes, season well and serve it neatly. Spread extra prawn mixture on top and garnish with browned shallots, shredded chillies and sliced egg. Serve lime wedges and gravy separately.

Mee Rebus

(Yellow Noodles in Curry Gravy)

Preparation time 1 hr • *Cooking time* 2 hr • *Serves* 4–6

Coriander seeds 1 Tbsp
Dried red chillies 15, soaked to soften
Shallots 20
Water 8½ cups
Tamarind pulp 1 Tbsp
Lean beef 600 g
Beef stock 5 cups
Cloves 2
Cinnamon stick 5-cm length
Sweet potatoes 600 g, boiled and mashed
Salt 2 tsp
Cooking oil 2 Tbsp
Firm bean curd (*pak towfoo*) 2 pieces
Bean sprouts 1 cup, tailed
Thick yellow noodles 600 g
Eggs 2, hard-boiled, shelled and sliced
Tomatoes 2, sliced
Green chillies 2, sliced
Spring onions 2, chopped
Limes 2, cut into wedges

1. Roast the coriander seeds in a pan over low heat and pound until fine. Grind together soften dried chillies and 10 shallots. Slice the remaining shallots. Add $^1/_2$ cup water to the tamarind to extract the juice.

2. Boil the beef in 6 cups water. When it boils, lower the heat and allow to simmer for 1–1½ hours until the beef is tender. Remove beef, cool and cut into thin slices.

3. To the beef stock, add the ground ingredients, pounded coriander, cloves and cinnamon and allow the stock to boil gently for about 10 minutes. Add mashed sweet potatoes, salt and tamarind juice to the stock. Cook until fairly thick and season to taste.

4. Heat cooking oil and fry the bean curd until brown on the outside. Remove to a cutting board and cut each piece into 8 pieces. Brown the sliced shallots and keep for garnishing.

5. Boil the remaining water and blanch the bean sprouts and then scald the noodles. Drain well.

6. Lay equal amounts of blanched bean sprouts in each serving bowl. Spread the noodles over the bean sprouts. Lay sliced meat over the noodles and pour hot gravy over. Garnish with sliced egg, bean curd, tomato slices, browned shallots, green chilli and spring onion. Serve with the lime wedges.

Mee Rebus (Yellow Noodles in Curry Gravy)

Fried Mee, Cantonese Style

Fried Mee, Cantonese Style

Preparation time 20–25 min • *Cooking time* 10–15 min • *Serves* 2–3

Freshwater prawns 4, medium-sized
Lean pork 150 g
Pig's liver 100 g
Threadfin (*ikan kurau*) 100 g
Flowering cabbage (*choy sum*) 6 stalks
Light soy sauce 2 tsp
A shake of pepper
Tapioca flour $^1/_2$ tsp
Salt $^1/_2$ tsp
Water 1 cup
Sugar $^1/_4$ tsp
Sesame oil $^1/_2$ tsp
Fried egg noodles (*yee mien*) 225 g
Cooking oil $^1/_2$ cup
Shallots 3, sliced
Garlic 2 cloves, chopped
Tapioca flour mixture blended from
    1 tsp tapioca flour and $^1/_4$ cup water
Egg 1, beaten

1. Wash prawns and halve lengthwise. Slice pork, liver and fish. Use only the young shoots of flowering cabbage and leave them whole. Season pork with $^1/_2$ tsp light soy sauce and a shake of pepper. Season liver with $^1/_2$ tsp tapioca flour, $^1/_2$ tsp light soy sauce and a shake of pepper.

2. Mix ingredients for gravy: to the water, add the remaining light soy sauce, $^1/_4$ tsp salt, sugar, sesame oil and a good shake of pepper.

3. Place noodles in a large bowl and pour boiling water over. As soon as noodles appear limp, drain well. Heat 2 Tbsp cooking oil and fry softened noodles for 3–4 minutes. Lay noodles on a serving dish, spreading out as flat as possible.

4. Heat 1 Tbsp cooking oil and brown shallots and garlic. Add prawns and pork and fry for a minute until the colour changes. Add the gravy mixture, cover and cook for 3–4 minutes. Add flowering cabbage, liver and fish and as soon as the gravy boils again, thicken with tapioca flour mixture. Season gravy to taste and turn off the heat.

5. Add egg to the gravy quickly, then pour gravy over the fried noodles. Sprinkle pepper and serve with pickled chillies.

Note: Any kind of meat can be substituted for pork and liver and any other seafood may be used in place of prawns and threadfin (*ikan kurau*). Allow 80–100 g of fried egg noodles (*yee mien*) per person.

Vegetarian Fried Beehoon

Preparation time 25 min • *Cooking time* 20 min • *Serves* 4

Cooking oil 3 Tbsp
Hard bean curd slices (*teem chok*)
    3 pieces, cut into thin strips with
    kitchen scissors
Dried Chinese mushrooms 4, soaked
    and shredded
Carrot 1, shredded
Salt $^1/_2$ tsp
Light soy sauce 1 Tbsp
Dark soy sauce $^1/_2$ tsp
Water 1 cup
Rice vermicelli 200 g, soaked to soften
Cabbage 8–10 leaves, shredded
Flowering cabbage (*choy sum*) 4 stalks,
    cut into 4-cm lengths
Bean sprouts 2 cups, tailed
Spring onion 1, cut into 4-cm lengths
Chilli 1, shredded

1. Heat cooking oil and fry hard bean curd strips over a very low fire until lightly browned. Remove to a dish.

2. In the same oil, fry shredded mushrooms and carrot. Add salt, light and dark soy sauce and water, followed by softened vermicelli. Stir to mix well before adding cabbage and flowering cabbage.

3. See that the ingredients are well mixed and cooked. Cooked rice vermicelli is limp, yet retains its firmness. Overcooked rice vermicelli expands and is mushy. Add bean sprouts, fried hard bean curd strips and spring onion. Toss for a minute to mix well and to cook the vegetables. Season and serve garnished with shredded chilli.

**Hard Bean Curd Slices
(*Teem Chok*)**

Seasoned, brown rectangular pieces of dried soy bean curd. These are used mainly in vegetarian cooking.

Wonton Mee

Preparation time 40 min • *Cooking time* 20 min • *Serves* 4

Water chestnuts or yam bean
   (*bangkuang*) 1 Tbsp, finely diced
Ginger 1-cm knob
Flowering cabbage (*choy sum*) 150 g
BBQ pork (*char siew*) 300 g
Pork 100 g, minced
Spring onion 2 tsp, chopped
Tapioca flour 1 tsp
Salt 1 tsp
Light soy sauce 3 tsp
Sesame oil 1 tsp
Egg white 1, beaten
A shake of pepper
Wonton skins 25 pieces
Cooking oil 2 Tbsp
Shallots 3, sliced
Stock 6 cups
Water 6 cups
Oyster sauce 2 tsp
Fresh fine egg noodles 350 g

EXTRA SEASONING FOR SERVING
Vegetable oil 1 Tbsp
Sesame oil 1 tsp
Oyster sauce 2 tsp
Light soy sauce 1 tsp
A shake of pepper

1. Cut off 2 thin slices of ginger and pound the rest to extract ginger juice. Pluck young shoots of flowering cabbage and leave them whole. Cut BBQ pork into 1-cm thick slices.

2. Mix minced pork with water chestnuts or yam bean, ginger juice, spring onion, tapioca flour, 1/2 tsp salt, 1 tsp light soy sauce, 1/2 tsp sesame oil, egg white and a good shake of pepper. Knead well to mix the ingredients thoroughly. Spread out a wonton skin and place a teaspoonful of this filling in the centre. Press wonton skin together to enclose filling completely.

3. Heat 1 Tbsp cooking oil and brown the shallot and ginger slices. Add the stock with the remaining salt and light soy sauce and a good shake of pepper. Keep the stock hot.

4. In a saucepan, boil water and add the wontons and cook for 4 minutes or until they float. Lift the cooked wontons from the boiling water and plunge them into a basin of cold water. Drain well and keep aside.

5. Prepare 4 serving bowls: in each bowl, place 1/4 Tbsp vegetable oil, 1/4 tsp sesame oil, 1/2 tsp oyster sauce, 1/4 tsp light soy sauce and a shake of pepper.

6. Allow the water in the saucepan to come to a boil again. Loosen the strands of a quarter portion of noodles and drop it into the boiling water. Stir with chopsticks and cook for 1 minute. Use a large slotted spoon to lift the noodles from the boiling water and plunge them, still in the spoon, into a basin of cold water. Remove, shake out excess water and plunge into the boiling water again. Lift out at once, drain well and place in one of the 4 prepared serving bowls. Use a pair of chopsticks or a fork to mix in the seasoning thoroughly.

7. Boil flowering cabbage lightly in boiling stock. When cooked, remove to a dish.

8. To serve, place some flowering cabbage, wontons and sliced BBQ pork over the noodles in each bowl before pouring boiling stock over. Serve with pickled green chillies.

Note: Instead of BBQ pork (*char siew*), other meats may be used. Cooked egg noodles must be plunged into cold water to stop further cooking. If this is not done, the noodles will become very soft and starchy. If fresh egg noodles are not available, use dried egg noodles. Measure approximately 300 g. Soak dried noodles for 10–15 minutes to soften. Cook exactly as for fresh noodles, but double the cooking time.

Wonton Skins (*Wonton Pei*)

These are paper-thin squares of egg noodle dough, about 7.5-cm wide. They are usually available wherever fresh egg noodle is sold. The round ones shown are *sui kow* skins.

Har Mee

(Yellow Noodles in Prawn Soup)

Preparation time 1 hr • *Cooking time* 1¹/₂ hr • *Serves* 4–6

Spareribs 600 g
Water 11 cups
Lean pork 300 g
Prawns 300 g, medium-sized
Dried sole 1, deboned
Salt 1 tsp
Light soy sauce 2 tsp
Cooking oil 5 Tbsp
Shallots ¹/₂ cup, sliced
Ground chilli 1 Tbsp
Bean sprouts 150 g, tailed
Yellow noodles 500 g
Water convolvulus (*kangkung*) 300 g,
    plucked to 5-cm lengths

1. Boil spareribs in 8 cups water. When boiling, add lean pork. When it boils again, lower heat and allow soup to simmer for 1–1¹/₂ hours. Take out lean pork after ¹/₂ hour and cool before slicing. Remove spareribs only after 1–1¹/₂ hours.

2. Bring stock to a boil again and add prawns. When they are cooked, about 3 minutes, remove and shell. Halve shelled prawns lengthwise. Return shells and bones of dried sole to the stock and simmer for another 30 minutes. Strain and allow to boil again. Season to taste with salt and light soy sauce.

3. Heat cooking oil and brown sliced shallots. Remove brown shallots to a small bowl. Fry deboned sole over slow fire until brown and crisp. Remove from pan and pound until fine.

4. Mix ground chilli with sufficient water to make a paste. Fry this paste in the same oil, adding more oil if necessary until chilli is dark. Remove to a small dish. In the same pan, fry sliced prawns for 2 minutes until they curl up and are evenly coated with chilli oil.

5. Boil the remaining water and scald bean sprouts, followed by noodles. Drain well. Blanch water convolvulus lightly.

6. Divide and place bean sprouts, water convolvulus, noodles, pork and prawns in this order into 4–6 bowls. Ladle hot soup over and garnish with powdered sole and shallots. Serve with chilli *sambal*.

Note: For a more flavoured soup, pound prawn shells and place in a sieve. Stand sieve in a bowl filled with a little water. Rub as much of the pounded shell through as possible. Add this liquid to the soup to 'thicken' it. However, some people find this too fishy for their taste.

Lam Mee (Penang Birthday Noodles)

Lam Mee

(Penang Birthday Noodles)

Preparation time 30–40 min • *Cooking time* 20 min • *Serves* 4–5

Cooking oil 3 Tbsp
Shallots 1 cup, sliced
Garlic 1 Tbsp, chopped
Eggs 2, beaten with a pinch of salt
  and a shake of pepper
Water 3 cups
Pork or chicken meat 200 g
Dark soy sauce 1/2 tsp
Prawns 300 g, medium, shelled and
  sliced in half lengthwise
Light soy sauce 2 tsp
Salt and pepper to taste
Tapioca flour 1 tsp, blended with
  1 Tbsp water
Bean sprouts 2 cups, tailed
Flowering cabbage (*choy sum*) 8 stalks
Fresh egg noodles 500 g
Crabmeat 1 cup
Red chillies 2, shredded
Coriander leaves 1 sprig, chopped

1. Heat cooking oil in a wok and brown the sliced shallots. Drain on kitchen paper and keep for garnishing. Brown chopped garlic. Drain and keep for garnishing. Remove excess oil from wok and keep it for use later.

2. Heat up the greased wok and make very thin omelettes from the egg mixture. Roll up each omelette as it is made. Finely shred the omelettes for garnishing. Set aside.

3. Heat water in a saucepan and boil the pork or chicken meat for 4–5 minutes. Cool the meat before shredding it finely. Reserve the stock for making the gravy.

4. Return the cooking oil used for frying the shallots and garlic to the wok, heat it up and fry the shredded boiled meat. Add dark soy sauce and cook for another minute before adding in the prawns. Add the stock and light soy sauce, and simmer for 5 minutes to get good gravy. Season the gravy with salt and pepper before thickening it with the tapioca flour mixture. Keep the gravy hot over a low heat.

5. Boil 1/2 saucepan of water and blanch the bean sprouts, flowering cabbage and egg noodles separately. Using a large serving dish, spread the bean sprouts evenly on the dish. Cover the bean sprouts with a layer of noodles. Cut the cooked flowering cabbage into 4-cm lengths and spread them over the noodles.

6. Pour the hot gravy over the noodles and spread the crabmeat, browned onions and garlic on top. Garnish with shredded omelette, chilli and coriander leaves. Serve immediately with *sambal belacan (spicy shrimp paste).

*Sambal Belacan (Spicy Shrimp Paste)

Red chillies 5
Bird's eye chillies (*cili padi*) 5
Dried shrimp paste (*belacan*)
  3 x 3 x 0.5-cm piece, roasted
Kaffir lime leaves (*daun limau purut*)
  3, finely shredded
Small limes (*limau kesturi*) 2

1. Pound chillies with the hot roasted dried shrimp paste to make the *sambal*. Add shredded lime leaves and lime juice to the *sambal*.

2. This *sambal* can be served with most Malaysian dishes.

Fried Hokkien Mee

Preparation time 20 min • Cooking time 10–15 min • Serves 4

Pork 100 g
Prawns 150 g, medium-sized
Squid (optional) 3, medium-sized
Flowering cabbage (*choy sum*) 4 stalks
Cabbage 500–600 g
Dark soy sauce 1 Tbsp
Light soy sauce 1 Tbsp
Sugar ¹/₂ tsp
Salt ¹/₂ tsp
Stock 2 cups
Cooking oil 5 Tbsp
Garlic 6 cloves, chopped
Thick yellow noodles 500 g
A shake of pepper

1. Slice pork, shell and devein prawns, clean squid (optional) and cut them into 1-cm thick slices. Clean and pluck flowering cabbage into 4-cm lengths. Wash and cut cabbage into 3 cm wide pieces. Mix dark and light soy sauce, sugar and salt in the stock for a gravy mixture.

2. Heat cooking oil in a pan and brown the garlic. Add pork and fry for a minute until it changes colour, then add prawns and squid (optional) and fry for another minute before adding the gravy mixture.

3. When the gravy mixture boils, add the noodles and vegetables. Cover pan for 3–4 minutes. Mix well and keep turning the noodles over until most of the gravy is absorbed. Season to taste and serve with a good shake of pepper.

4. Serve Fried Hokkien Mee with *sambal belacan* (spicy shrimp paste) (refer to page 123) or fresh sliced chillies in light soy sauce.

Note: Rice vermicelli or rice noodles (*kway teow*) may be substituted for *Hokkien mee* or thick noodles. Mussels may also be added to this dish. *Hokkien Mee* is sometimes served with a slight well made in the centre of the noodles and a raw egg broken into this well. The heat from the noodles below cooks the egg very lightly.

Wat Dan Hor

(Beef Fried with Flat Rice Noodles)

Preparation time 20 min • Cooking time 10 min • Serves 4–5

Cooking oil 2 Tbsp
Shallots 2, chopped
Garlic 1 clove, chopped
Flat rice noodles (*hor fun/kwai teow*)
    500 g, rubbed together to loosen folds
Fillet steak 200–300 g, sliced thinly
Light soy sauce 2 tsp
Tapioca flour 2 tsp
Young ginger 6–7-cm piece, sliced
Water or stock 1¹/₂ cups
Flowering cabbage (*choy sum*) 3 stalks,
    plucked into 4–5-cm pieces
Spring onions 2, cut into 4-cm lengths
Egg 1, beaten with a pinch of salt and
    a shake of pepper
Salt to taste

1. Heat up 1 Tbsp cooking oil in a wok and lightly brown shallots and garlic. Add the noodles and toss together for 2 minutes. Add in 1 tsp light soy sauce. When noddles begin to look limp, it is ready. Remove to a serving dish and keep warm.

2. Marinade the sliced steak with the remaining light soy sauce and tapioca flour.

3. Add remaining cooking oil to the wok and fry the sliced ginger for 1 minute. Add the seasoned steak and mix well. Add the water or stock and flowering cabbage. Cook for 1 minute then turn off the heat before adding the spring onions and beaten egg.

4. Season to taste and pour the meat and gravy over the fried noodles. Serve immediately with pickled green chillies.

Desserts
and Snacks

Pulut Tai-Tai (Glutinous Rice Cakes) with Serikaya (Egg Custard)

Pulut Tai-Tai
(Glutinous Rice Cakes)
Preparation time 3 hr • *Cooking time* 40–50 min

Glutinous rice 300 g
Coconut $1/2$, grated
Water $2^1/_2$ cups
Butterfly or blue pea flowers
   (*bunga telang*) (optional) 24–30
Pandan (screwpine) leaves 2
Salt $1/_4$ tsp
A piece of banana leaf,
greaseproof paper or tin foil

1. Wash and soak glutinous rice for at least 3 hours. Extract coconut cream from the grated coconut without adding water. Then add 2 cups water to the grated coconut to get the coconut milk. Wash and pound the butterfly or blue pea flowers and extract the juice. If less than 1 tsp juice is obtained, add 1 tsp water to the flowers and try to get more juice. If water has to be added, add 2–3 drops of colouring to help deepen the colour. Alternatively, use blue food colouring in place of butterfly or blue pea flowers if unavailable.

2. Drain glutinous rice and put it into the prepared steaming tray with the coconut milk and pandan leaves. Steam the rice over boiling water for 20–30 minutes until the rice is cooked. Remove the rice from the steamer and add in the coconut cream and salt. With a fork or a pair of chopsticks, mix the rice and coconut cream well together. Colour about one-third portion of the rice blue with the colouring then return the rice to steam for another 10 minutes.

3. Remove the rice from the steamer when it is well cooked. Spoon the rice into a loaf tin that has been rinsed with water, alternating the blue and the white rice.

4. With a piece of folded banana leaf or greaseproof paper, level off the top and press the rice down as much as possible. Cover the top with the piece of banana leaf, greaseproof paper or tin foil and place something very heavy on it to weigh down the rice.

5. When the rice has cooled, cut into slices and serve with Serikaya (Egg Custard).

Kuih Bengka
(Custard Cake)
Preparation time 20 min • *Cooking time* 1 hr

Coconut 1, grated
Rice flour 1 cup
Green pea (*hoon kway*) flour 2 Tbsp
Sugar 1 cup
Salt $1/_2$ tsp
Pandan (screwpine) leaves 2
Banana leaf 1

1. Without adding water to the grated coconut, extract coconut cream. Then add water and extract 2 cups coconut milk.

2. Knead rice flour, green pea flour and sugar with the coconut cream until sugar is dissolved. Add salt and enough liquid from the coconut milk to get $2^1/_2$ cups batter.

3. Strain batter through a fine hair sieve into a large saucepan. Cook batter with the pandan leaves in it, stirring all the time with a wooden spoon until it thickens and bubbles.

4. Pour cooked custard into a 20-cm square tin lined with softened banana leaf. Level off the top and bake in a hot oven (200°C) for 1 hour until the top and sides are well browned.

5. Cool Kuih Bengka thoroughly before cutting into 1-cm slices for serving.

Note: To soften banana leaves, hold them over a heat for a minute or until they change colour.

Serikaya
(Egg Custard)

Preparation time 40–50 min • *Cooking time* 3–4 hr

Coconut 1¹/₂, grated
Eggs 4, medium
Sugar 2 cups
Pandan (screwpine) leaves 3

1. Extract coconut cream without adding any water to the grated coconut.

2. Beat the eggs and sugar in a heatproof container until sugar dissolves. Add coconut cream and mix well. The container holding the custard must not be allowed to come into direct contact with heat, so place it on a metal stand in a much larger pot of boiling water to steam. Steam uncovered for 1 hour, stirring continuously. After that, cover both containers and allow the custard to steam over vigorously boiling water for 2 hours. Add more boiling water to the larger pot every ¹/₂ hour and at the same time stir the custard well.

3. After 3 hours' steaming, the mixture should be golden brown. Add pandan leaves and allow it to finish steaming for another hour without stirring. Cool before filling into clean, warm bottles.

4. Serve Serikaya with Pulut Tai-Tai (Glutinous Rice Cakes).

Note: Water must never be allowed to drip into the Serikaya. To prevent condensation forming under the lid of the Serikaya container, fold an absorbent cloth such as muslin a few times so that it is thick but still larger than the lid and place it over the container before putting the lid on. The cloth will absorb condensing steam. When cooling the custard after steaming, remove the lid.

Microwaved Serikaya
(Microwaved Egg Custard)

Preparation time 10 min • *Cooking time* 8–10

This microwaved version is an alternative to the traditional one. Both are equally delicious. Serikaya goes well with Pulut Tai-Tai (refer to page 127) or bread.

Eggs 7, large
Sugar 500 g
Coconut cream (*pati santan*) 2 cups
Caramel colouring (optional) 2–3 drops
Pandan (screwpine) leaf 1

1. Whisk together eggs and sugar until sugar is thoroughly dissolved. Add coconut cream and strain mixture into a microwave-safe dish. Cover dish with microwave-safe cling wrap, but leave a breathing vent of about 5 cm on one side.

2. Cook mixture in a microwave oven at moderate heat for 2 minutes. Take it out, whisk it well and return it to the microwave oven to cook for another 2 minutes. Whisk it again to remove any lumpiness, add colouring, if desired. Put the pandan leaf into the mixture and cook for another 2 minutes. Remove pandan leaf from mixture.

3. Whisk again until smooth, and check consistency. If it is still a little watery, cook a further 1–2 minutes, as required. Cool Serikaya before bottling and store in fridge.

Pulut Inti

(Steamed Glutinous Rice with Sweet Coconut Topping)

Preparation time 30 min • Cooking time 25 min

Glutinous rice 300 g
Banana leaves 8 pieces
(each 20-cm wide)
Pandan (screwpine) leaves 2
Coconut $1/_2$, grated
Salt $1/_4$ tsp
Palm sugar (*gula melaka*) 4 Tbsp
Granulated sugar 1 Tbsp
Water 3 Tbsp

1. Wash and soak glutinous rice for at least 4 hours. Soften the banana leaves by scalding. Shred pandan leaves lengthwise and tie into a knot.

2. Extract 1 cup coconut milk from half the grated coconut. Drain soaked glutinous rice and place it in a steaming tray with salt, coconut milk and knotted pandan leaves. Steam rice for 20–25 minutes until it is well cooked. Discard the pandan leaves.

3. Melt palm sugar and granulated sugar with water and add the rest of the grated coconut to it. Cook coconut until it is soft and dry. Cool it on a plate.

4. Spoon 1 Tbsp cooked rice onto each piece of softened banana leaf, place 1 tsp cooked coconut on top of it and wrap around it neatly. Serve.

Shanghai Pancakes

Shanghai Pancakes

Preparation time 40–50 min • *Cooking time* 25–30 min

Cooking oil 3 Tbsp
Sesame seeds

BEAN PASTE
Red beans 300 g, soaked overnight
Sugar 120–180 g
Cooking oil 4 Tbsp

BATTER
Plain flour 1 cup
A pinch of salt
Egg 1, beaten
Water 1 cup

1. Make bean paste: boil soaked red beans in a pressure cooker for $1/2$ hour. Mash softened beans and pass them through a sieve to remove the tough skin. Pour this puree into a calico bag and hang it up to enable water to drain away. Turn out bean paste onto a frying pan and cook over low heat with sugar and cooking oil. Keep stirring the paste to prevent burning. When paste is ready, it should be very smooth and glossy. This paste can be made beforehand and kept in a fridge for up to 10 days.

2. Make batter: sieve plain flour and salt into a bowl. Make a well in the centre, put the egg and $1/2$ cup water in the well and mix to get a smooth batter. Beat batter for 10 minutes and then add the rest of the water. Let batter stand for $1/2$ hour.

3. Fry pancakes in a hot, greased pan until they are lightly browned on both sides. Turn pancakes out onto a plate, spread bean paste on it and fold the top and bottom over to get a long, rectangular-shaped cake that completely covers the bean paste.

4. When all the pancakes have been filled and folded over, heat 2 Tbsp cooking oil in a frying pan and fry each pancake again until it is well-browned. Cut each pancake into 2.5-cm pieces and serve sprinkled with sesame seeds.

Note: This pancake is sometimes served with Peanut Cream.

Coconut Cream

Preparation time 30 min • *Cooking time* 25 min

Coconut $1/2$, grated
Sugar 6 Tbsp
Gelatine 3 tsp, dissolved in $1/2$ cup
   warm water
Evaporated milk $1/2$ cup, chilled
Desiccated coconut 1 Tbsp
Glace cherries 2–3, halved

1. Add a little boiled, cooled water and extract 1 cup coconut milk from the grated coconut. Place coconut milk in a large mixing bowl standing in a basin of ice. Add sugar and stir until sugar dissolves. Add liquid gelatine and stir until mixture thickens.

2. Add cold evaporated milk to mixture and whisk briskly until it resembles whipped cream. Pour into a serving bowl and chill in the fridge until it sets.

3. To serve, sprinkle desiccated coconut on top and decorate with cherries.

Peanut Cream

Preparation time 30 min • *Cooking time* 25 min

Peanuts $1/2$ cup, dry roasted and skinned
Sesame seeds 1 Tbsp, dry roasted
Water $3 1/2$ cups
Sugar 6 Tbsp
Cornflour 1 rounded Tbsp, blended with
   $1 1/2$ Tbsp water
Evaporated milk $1/4$ cup

1. Place peanuts, sesame seeds and 1 cup water in a blender. Blend at high speed until smooth. Strain mixture thorough a sieve into a saucepan, adding the rest of the water to help strain the mixture. Boil the mixture over moderate heat and add sugar. When it boils again, thicken with cornflour mixture. Remove pan from heat and mix in the evaporated milk. Serve hot.

Agar-Agar Gula Goreng
(Caramel Jelly)
Preparation time 5 min • *Cooking time* 25–30 min

Agar-agar strips or powder 5 g (strips)
or 1¼ tsp (powder)
Water 2 cups + 5 Tbsp
Sugar 2 Tbsp
Egg yolk 1
Evaporated milk ¼ cup
Granulated sugar ½ cup

1. Combine agar-agar strips or powder and 2 cups water. Add sugar and boil until sugar dissolves. Strain the mixture. Beat egg yolk with evaporated milk and stir this into the agar-agar mixture.

2. To make the caramel, put granulated sugar and 5 Tbsp water in a heavy pan and cook over very low heat. Stir constantly and do not allow the solution to come to a boil until all the sugar has dissolved. When the sugar has dissolved, increase the heat, stop stirring and allow to boil until it is a deep golden colour.

3. Stir the agar-agar mixture into the caramel over medium heat. When the caramel and agar-agar are thoroughly mixed, pour into a mould and chill to set.

4. When the agar-agar has set, turn it out and serve with mixed fruit.

Agar-Agar (*Tai Choy Koh*)

A seaweed used widely in Southeast Asia for making jellies. It has better setting qualities than gelatine and can set without refrigeration. It is available in strips or powder form from Chinese grocery stores or supermarkets.

Agar-Agar Ubi Santan
(Sweet Potato and Coconut Milk Jelly)
Preparation time 30 min • *Cooking time* 20 min

Sweet potato 300–400 g of white variety
Agar-agar strips or powder 10 g (strips)
or 2½ tsp (powder)
Water 4 cups
Pandan (screwpine) leaves 2
Sugar ½ cup
Yellow food colouring 2–3 drops
Coconut ½, grated
Cocoa powder 2 tsp

1. Scrub and boil the sweet potato. When it is cooked, skin and mash it by passing through a sieve to remove the fibre.

2. Add agar-agar strips or powder to water in a saucepan and boil with pandan leaves until agar-agar dissolves. Add sugar and stir to dissolve the sugar, then strain the liquid.

3. Mix a little less than half the agar-agar mixture with mashed sweet potato, add a few drops of yellow food colouring, and pour it into a mould. Chill to set.

4. Without adding water to the grated coconut, extract coconut cream. This should be done quickly and be ready while the remaining agar-agar is still hot. Stir the coconut cream into the remaining agar-agar and keep it warm so that it does not set.

5. When the yellow layer of agar-agar has set, scratch its surface with a fork and pour a 1-cm layer of white agar-agar on top of it. Chill to set the second layer.

6. In the meantime, blend cocoa powder with 1 Tbsp water. Add the blended cocoa to the rest of the agar-agar and boil it to cook the cocoa. When the white layer has set, scratch its surface and pour brown agar-agar over it. Chill once again to set then turn out to serve.

Almond Jelly and Fruit

Preparation time 5 min • *Cooking time* 15 min

Agar-agar strips or powder 10 g (strips)
    or 2 tsp (powder)
Water 6 cups
Evaporated milk $^1/_2$ cup
Sugar $^1/_2$ cup
Almond essence $^1/_2$ tsp
Pineapple 1
Granulated sugar $^1/_2$ cup

1. Add agar-agar strips or powder to 4 cups water in a pan and boil until agar-agar dissolves. Add evaporated milk and sugar and boil again until the sugar dissolves. Stir in almond essence and strain the liquid into a tray. Chill to set.

2. Remove the hard core of the pineapple and dice pineapple into 3-cm cubes. Boil the remaining water with granulated sugar. When it boils, add pineapple cubes and allow them to stew for 5 minutes. Remove from heat, cool and refrigerate.

3. When the jelly has set, cut into 2.5-cm cubes. Serve it and pineapple cubes chilled in pineapple syrup.

Note: Canned lychees, longans, fruit cocktail and watermelon balls may be used either with, or in place of, the pineapple.

Mah Tai Kung
(Water Chestnut in Syrup)

Preparation time 20 min • *Cooking time* 5 min • *Serves* 5–6

Water chestnuts 300 g, skinned
Water 4 cups
Rock sugar 100 g
Egg 1, beaten

1. Put water chestnuts and 2 cups water in a blender. Blend for 30 seconds, just long enough to break up the water chestnuts.

2. Boil remaining water with rock sugar until sugar dissolves. Add blended water chestnuts and bring to boil. The mixture should be lightly thickened. Taste for sweetness.

3. Turn off the heat and drizzle the beaten egg into the mixture stirring all the time so that ribbons of egg are formed. This is a very refreshing dessert after a meal or a refreshing snack on a hot day. It can be served hot or cold.

Pak Koh Fu Chok Tong Sui
(Ginko Nut and Bean Curd Skin in Syrup)

Preparation time 30 min • *Cooking time* 50–60 min • *Serves* 5–6

Ginko nuts 200 g
Water 2 litres
Dried bean curd skin (*fu chok*) 2, soaked
Pandan (screwpine) leaves 2
Rock or granulated sugar 200 g

1. Crack the ginko nuts with a hammer or nutcracker, and peel away the brown skin. Put the ginko nuts and water in a saucepan and bring it to the boil. Cover and simmer for 30 minutes to soften the nuts.

2. Add the soaked bean curd sticks and simmer for another 20–30 minutes until the they break up into flakes about 1.5-cm long. Add the pandan leaves and the rock sugar and boil until the sugar dissolves.

3. Taste for sweetness and add more sugar, if necessary. This makes a delightful tea-time snack.

Note: The ginko nuts can be shelled and skinned in advance and kept in the fridge for a day or two. Dried bean curd stick (*fu chok*) must be used as soon as possible after opening. If kept for more than a month, it will not soften or break up when boiled, but will remain as tough pieces.

Dried Bean Curd Skin

Dried bean curd skin can be found in stick (*fu chok*) or sheet (*fu pei*) form. Dried bean curd skins are thin, yellow pieces of skin formed on the top of soy bean milk before it coagulates. Dried bean curd stick is commonly used in desserts.

Kuih Jagung
(Cream Corn Cake)

Preparation time 20 min • *Cooking time* 8–10 min • *Serves* 4

Coconut $^1/_2$, grated
Green pea (*hoon kway*) flour 50 g
Sugar $^3/_4$ cup
A pinch of salt
Pandan (screwpine) leaves (optional) 2
Creamed corn 1 cup
Food colouring 2–3 drops

1. Extract $2^1/_2$ cups coconut milk from the grated coconut.

2. Blend green pea flour, sugar, salt and coconut milk in a pan, making sure that there are no lumps of flour. Add pandan leaves or a few drops of vanilla essence and cook the mixture over a medium heat, stirring all the time until it bubbles. Add creamed corn and food colouring. Stir for a minute, then pour into 4 sundae glasses. Chill well before serving.

Note: The mixture can be set in a tray and cut into pieces before serving. Alternatively, make boats or baskets with banana leaves which have been softened by scalding and set the mixture in them.

Pandan (Screwpine) Leaves (*Daun Pandan* or *Lum Pei Yip*)

These are stiff, long and narrow dark green leaves with a pronounced furrow down its centre. When cooked with food, it imparts a lovely aroma and flavour. The leaves are also pounded and the green juice extracted to be added to food for colour and flavour.

Lime Cordial

Preparation time 30 min • *Cooking time* 15 min

Water 1 cup
Granulated sugar 3 cups
Small limes (*limau kesturi*) 500 g

1. Boil the water and sugar together until the sugar dissolves. Cool the syrup.

2. Squeeze the juice from the limes and strain into a sterile cordial bottle. Add the cool syrup to it and cover tightly.

3. Shake the bottle to mix the cordial thoroughly. Store in fridge. This cordial is refreshing and thirst quenching.

Pineapple Tarts

Pineapple Tarts

Preparation time 1¹/₂ hr • *Cooking time* 30 min • *Makes* 60

Plain flour 2 cups
Salt ¹/₂ tsp
Margarine 10 Tbsp, cold
Egg yolk 1
Cold water 2 Tbsp
Egg white 1, beaten
Pineapple jam (recipe on the right) 1 cup

1. Sieve plain flour and salt together into a bowl. Cut margarine into flour until it is in small pieces. Using fingertips, rub margarine quickly into the flour until there are no big lumps. Beat egg yolk with cold water and add it to the flour. Mix until pastry binds together. If necessary, add a little more cold water.

2. Sprinkle a little flour on a clean, smooth tabletop or a pastry board. Dip a tart cutter of about 2.5-cm diameter in the flour. Working with a large handful of pastry at a time, knead lightly on the working surface and roll out to 0.5-cm thickness. With the floured tart cutter, cut out the rounds as closely as possible. Make a very slight depression of about 1.25-cm diameter in the centre of each round of pastry. Fill this with pineapple jam. Decorate the edge with pastry pincers.

3. Decorate the tarts with bits of leftover pastry.

4. Brush the tarts with beaten egg white and bake in a moderately hot oven (190°C) for 25–30 minutes or until pastry is cooked and evenly browned. Cool tarts on a wire tray before storing or serving.

Pineapple Jam

Preparation time 30 min • *Cooking time* 1 hr

Not-too-ripe pineapples 4
Cinnamon stick 7–8-cm length
Cloves 6
Sugar

1. Skin pineapple and remove the eyes. Grate them in a circular motion so that there is not too much fibre. Leave the grated pineapple in a sieve for 10 minutes for pineapple juice to drain off. (Cool the juice in the refrigerator—it makes a refreshing drink.)

2. Measure grated pineapple pulp. For every 1¹/₂ cups pulp, use 1 cup sugar. Place pineapple pulp, cinnamon and cloves in a saucepan and allow to boil for about ¹/₂ hour to reduce water content. Boil over medium heat and stir frequently to prevent burning. When the pineapple looks dry, add the measured amount of sugar and cook very slowly, stirring all the while, until the jam is a golden colour and of the desired consistency. This takes from ¹/₂–1 hour.

3. Pour jam into warmed jars and cover immediately. Pineapple jam can be stored in the fridge for months.

Bubur Cha-Cha

(Sweet Potato and Yam Pudding)

Preparation time 30 min • *Cooking time* 25 min

Sweet potato 300 g
Yam 300 g
Coconut $^1/_2$, grated
Sugar 225 g
A pinch of salt
Pandan (screwpine) leaves 2

1. Peel and dice sweet potato and yam into 1-cm cubes. Steam the cubes for about 15 minutes until cooked.

2. Without adding water to the grated coconut, extract $^1/_2$ cup coconut cream. Then add some water and extract 3 cups coconut milk.

3. Place coconut milk, sugar, salt and pandan leaves in a saucepan and bring to a boil, then add the cooked yam and sweet potato. When the coconut milk boils again, add coconut cream. Remove the saucepan from heat as soon as the milk comes to a boil again.

4. Serve Bubur Cha-Cha hot or cold. If serving it cold, reduce coconut milk to 2 cups, chill cooked Bubur Cha-Cha and serve with crushed ice.

Cendol

(Rich Green Pea Flour Pudding)

Preparation time 30 min • *Cooking time* 25 min

Pandan (screwpine) leaves 10
Green food colouring 2–3 drops
Green pea (*look tow fun*) flour $^1/_2$ cup
Palm sugar (*gula melaka*) 5 Tbsp
Granulated sugar 1 Tbsp
Water $4^1/_2$ cups
Coconut 1, grated
A pinch of salt

1. Pound pandan leaves to extract pandan juice. Add sufficient water to pandan juice with green food colouring to make 2 cups. Mix green pea flour with the pandan juice. Cook this mixture over medium heat stirring continuously until it bubbles.

2. Place a cendol frame over a basin of cold water and ice cubes. Spoon the cooked pandan mixture onto the cendol frame and with a spatula, press it through the holes into the cold water. Drain off the water and chill the cendol.

3. Boil the palm sugar and granulated sugar with $^1/_2$ cup water to get syrup. Strain and cool the syrup.

4. Add the remaining water to the grated coconut and extract coconut milk. Add a good pinch of salt to the coconut milk.

5. To serve, place 1 Tbsp cendol into a small serving bowl, then add 1 Tbsp syrup and $^1/_4$ cup coconut milk. Top the bowl with ice shavings and serve at once.

Note: If pure green pea (*hoon kway*) flour is used, mix $2^1/_2$ cups of pandan juice to $^1/_2$ cup green pea flour.

Palm Sugar
(***Gula Melaka or Yea Tong***)

Cakes of dark brown sugar made from the sap of the coconut palm. Good quality palm sugar has a very strong flavour of coconut.

Kuih Bengka Ubi
(Tapioca Cake)

Preparation time 35-40 min • Cooking time 1½ hr

Coconut ³/₄, grated
Tapioca 450 g
Tapioca flour 1 Tbsp
Granulated sugar 180 g
Palm sugar (*gula melaka*) 5 Tbsp
A pinch of salt

1. Without adding water to the grated coconut, extract ¹/₂ cup coconut cream. Then add a little water and extract ¹/₂ cup coconut milk. Let coconut milk stand for ¹/₂ hour in the fridge and then skim off the top.

2. Peel and grate the tapioca. Mix grated tapioca, tapioca flour, granulated sugar, palm sugar, salt and 1 cup coconut milk (obtained by mixing extractions of coconut cream and milk) together to get a mixture that is fairly liquid in consistency and which does not stick to the palm when touched.

3. Pour the mixture into a well-greased, 20-cm square tray and bake in a moderate oven (190°C) for 1–1¹/₂ hours. Cool thoroughly before cutting into 1-cm slices to serve.

Kuih Kosui

(Sweet Rice Cake)

Preparation time 25 min • *Cooking time* 20 min

Sugar 1 cup (combine 8 Tbsp
  chopped palm sugar and
  granulated sugar)
Boiling water 1 cup
Rice flour $^3/_4$ cup
Tapioca flour 4 Tbsp
Alkali water (*kan sui*) 1 tsp
Coconut $^1/_3$, skinned and grated fine
A pinch of salt

1. Dissolve sugar in boiling water and cool the syrup.

2. Mix rice flour and tapioca flour together, then add in the cool syrup. Stir in enough water to get 2 cups batter. Add alkali water and strain batter through muslin.

3. Heat a 20-cm steaming tray, pour in batter, stirring all the while until it begins to thicken. Cover it and steam for 20 minutes.

4. Mix grated coconut with salt. When the cake is cool, cut it up neatly with a knife dipped in cold water and toss each piece in the grated coconut so that it is coated all over. Serve neatly.

Note: For green-coloured Kuih Kosui, leave out the palm sugar and add pandan juice with a few drops of green food colouring. When this batter is cooked in small Chinese wine cups, it is known as Kuih Lompang.

Kuih Rose

(Crispy Sweet Rose)

Preparation time 15 min • *Cooking time* 30 min • *Makes* 24

Coconut $^1/_4$, grated
Plain flour $^3/_4$ cup
Rice flour 4 Tbsp
Sugar 3 Tbsp
Egg 1, beaten
Cooking oil for deep-frying

1. Extract 1 cup coconut milk from grated coconut. Sieve both kinds of flour into a bowl, add sugar and mix well. Make a well in the centre, drop in the egg and half the coconut milk and mix to get a smooth batter. Add the remaining coconut milk, beat the batter for 10 minutes and then let it rest for $^1/_2$ hour.

2. Heat cooking oil for deep-frying and heat the Kuih Rose mould in oil.

3. When both oil and mould are hot, lift the mould, shake away excess oil and dip it into the batter so that the batter nearly reaches the top of the mould. The mould should be evenly coated with a thin layer of batter. Hold the mould in hot oil and shake it gently when the batter browns and hardens so that it comes away from the mould. Fry Kuih Rose until they are golden brown. Drain well and cool before storing in an airtight container or serving.

Kuih Lapis
(Layered Steamed Cake)
Preparation time 30 min • *Cooking time* 30 min

Coconut 1, grated
Water 1¹/₂ cups
Rice flour 1 cup
Tapioca flour 1 Tbsp
Cornflour 1 Tbsp
Granulated sugar 1 cup
Red and yellow food colouring
   2–3 drops each

1. Without adding water to the grated coconut, extract coconut cream. Add water and extract coconut milk.

2. Knead the flours with sugar and the coconut cream until sugar dissolves. Mix in enough liquid from the coconut milk to get 2 cups batter. Strain batter through muslin and divide it into 2 equal parts. Colour one part pink by adding red food colouring.

3. Heat a 20-cm steaming tray and steam a thin layer of pink batter for 5 minutes until it is cooked. Ladle a thin layer of white batter on top of the pink and steam it for 3 minutes. Continue steaming thin layers, alternating the pink with the white and making sure each layer is cooked before adding the next layer.

4. When just enough batter for one layer remains, colour it bright red by adding a little more red colouring and a little yellow colouring to it before spreading it over the steamed kuih.

Note: Make sure the steaming tray is absolutely level before ladling on the batter. If it slopes even slightly, the layers will not be even. Use different ladles for different colours and do not mix them or the colours may run.

141

Kuih Keria

(Sugar-coated Sweet Potato Rings)

Preparation time 40 min • *Cooking time* 25–30 min

Sweet potatoes 600 g
Plain flour 60 g
Tapioca flour 60 g
Sugar 120 g
Water 3 Tbsp
Cooking oil for deep-frying

1. Scrub sweet potatoes and boil them in their jackets. When sweet potatoes are cooked, peel and mash them. Pass mashed potato through a sieve to remove all fibre. Mix in flours and knead together to get a firm dough. If sweet potatoes are very dry, add a little water to make dough more manageable.

2. Turn dough onto a floured board and roll it into a long roll 5-cm in diameter. Cut the roll into 12 equal slices. Shape each slice into a round cake 1-cm thick. With the handle of a wooden spoon, make a hole in the centre of each cake. Fry sweet potato rings in hot cooking oil till they are golden brown. Drain them and set aside.

3. Strain off the oil left in the frying pan. Put sugar and water into the oily pan. Melt sugar and boil until a very thick syrup is obtained. The thick syrup should be covered with white, close bubbles when it is ready. Return the rings to the pan and toss them in syrup until they are well coated and sugar crystallizes. Serve neatly.

Note: Kuih Keria is also known as Potato Doughnut.

Kuih Kochi

(Glutinous Rice Cake with Sweet Coconut Filling)

Preparation time 30–35 min • *Cooking time* 20–25 min

Banana leaves 10 pieces

DOUGH
Glutinous rice flour $^3/_4$ cup
Sugar 1 Tbsp
Pandan (screwpine) juice $2^1/_2$ Tbsp

FILLING
Palm sugar (*gula melaka*) 4 Tbsp
Granulated sugar 1 Tbsp
Water 2 Tbsp
Coconut $^1/_4$, grated
Tapioca flour 1 tsp, blended with
    2 tsp water

1. Scald the banana leaf to soften, then fold into cones about 10-cm deep. Grease them well.

2. Make the filling: dissolve palm sugar and granulated sugar in water. Add grated coconut and cook until coconut is soft and dry. Add tapioca flour mixture to coconut to bind it. Cool the filling and shape into 10 even-sized balls.

3. Make the dough: knead glutinous rice flour with sugar and pandan juice to get a soft tacky dough. Divide dough into 10 portions.

4. Divide each portion of dough into 2 unequal halves. Take the bigger half and press it into the tip of the cone and up the sides. Put a portion of the filling into the hollow and cover with the smaller piece of dough. Fold cone over to get a good shape and a firm base. Steam the cones for 20 minutes over boiling water.

5. If the Kuih Kochi loses its shape during steaming, refold after cooking.

Note: Kuih Kochi can be plain white or blue in colour. Two-coloured Kuih Kochi—white and green or white and blue—make attractive desserts.

Kuih Talam
(Pandan Layered Cake)
Preparation time 45 min • *Cooking time* 40–50 min

Sugar $^3/_4$ cup
Water 1 cup
Pandan (screwpine) leaves 10,
  pounded to extract juice

GREEN LAYER
Rice flour $^1/_2$ cup
Tapioca flour 4 Tbsp
Green pea (*hoon kway*) flour 1 Tbsp
Alkali water (*kan sui*) 1 tsp
Green food colouring 2–3 drops

WHITE LAYER
Coconut $^1/_2$, grated
Rice flour $^1/_4$ cup
Green pea (*hoon kway*) flour 1 Tbsp
Salt $^1/_4$ tsp

1. Dissolve sugar in water to obtain syrup. Cool the syrup.

2. For the green layer: knead the rice, tapioca and green pea flours together. Mix in syrup and pandan juice and enough water to get 2 cups batter. Add alkali water and green colouring before straining through a piece of thin muslin.

3. For the white layer: extract 1 cup coconut milk from grated coconut. Mix rice flour and green pea flour with the coconut milk to get 1½ cups batter. Add salt and strain through a piece of muslin.

4. Heat a 20-cm steaming tray. Pour in green batter and stir over medium heat until batter begins to thicken and flecks can be seen floating in the batter. Cover and steam for 20 minutes, when the top should be bubbly.

5. Use a clean, damp, thin muslin to blot any remaining liquid from the surface of this green layer before gently pouring the white batter onto it. Cover and steam for 10 minutes over medium heat. When cooked, the white layer should be set but not wrinkled. Cool thoroughly before cutting.

Note: For a brown and white Kuih Talam, omit the pandan juice. Chop up $^1/_2$ piece palm sugar and mix it with enough granulated sugar to make $^3/_4$ cup.

Sago Pudding
Preparation time 40 min • *Cooking time* 5–8 min

Pearl sago 1$^1/_2$ cups
Egg white 1
Brandy 2 Tbsp
Palm sugar (*gula melaka*) 5 Tbsp,
  chopped
Granulated sugar 2 Tbsp
Water 1 cup
Coconut 1, grated
A pinch of salt

1. Wash and soak sago for 30 minutes. Drain sago and put in a large sieve. Pour boiling water over the sago until it looks transparent. Shake the sieve to remove water.

2. Whisk egg white with the brandy in it. Mix whisked egg white into sago and turn the mixture into a mould. Chill the sago.

3. Put palm sugar into a saucepan with granulated sugar and water to boil. Reduce the syrup to about 1 cup and strain it into a small jug. Cool to room temperature before serving.

4. Add a little boiled water to the grated coconut and extract 1 cup coconut milk. Add a pinch of salt to the milk and serve it in a jug.

5. When sago is well chilled, turn it out and serve with syrup and coconut milk.

Sago (*Sar Kok Mai*)

In this book, we use pearl sago, which is manufactured from sago flour obtained from the pith of the sago palm. Sago is available from supermarkets.

Ondeh-Ondeh Keledek (Coconut-coated Sweet Potato Balls)

Ondeh-Ondeh
(Coconut-coated Glutinous Rice Balls)
Preparation time 40 min • *Cooking time* 15–20 min

Pandan (screwpine) leaves 10
Water 2 Tbsp
Palm sugar (*gula melaka*) 4 Tbsp
Granulated sugar 3 tsp
Glutinous rice flour $3/4$ cup
Coconut $1/4$, grated, white
A pinch of salt

1. Pound pandan leaves until fine. Add water and strain the juice.

2. Chop palm sugar and mix it with the white sugar.

3. Mix the glutinous rice flour with pandan juice to get a stiff dough. If dough is crumbly and too dry, add a little water to bind the flour to get a stiff dough. Take a piece of dough the size of a marble, press it into a flat disc and cook it in a saucepan of boiling water. When it boils and floats, take it out, drain it and knead it into the uncooked dough to get a smooth and pliable dough.

4. Roll the dough into a long roll 2.5-cm in diameter and cut it into pieces the size of small marbles. With fingers, shape each piece into a cup and put some of the mixed sugar in the hollow. Draw dough together to close the mouth and shape into a ball.

5. Cook balls of dough in quickly boiling water until they float Drain them well and toss them in grated coconut mixed with a pinch of salt. Serve Ondeh-Ondeh in banana leaf baskets.

Ondeh-Ondeh Keledek
(Coconut-coated Sweet Potato Balls)
Preparation time 1 hr • *Cooking time* 6–8 min

Palm sugar (*gula melaka*) 4 Tbsp
Sugar 2 tsp
Coconut $1/4$, grated, white
A pinch of salt
Plain flour $1^1/2$ Tbsp
Tapioca flour 1 Tbsp
Sweet potatoes with white
centres 300 g
Pandan (screwpine) leaves 10,
    pounded finely
Water 1 Tbsp
Green food colouring 2–3 drops

1. Chop up the palm sugar and mix it with white sugar. Mix grated coconut with a pinch of salt. Sieve both kinds of flour.

2. Clean and boil sweet potatoes in their jackets until cooked. When cool, skin and mash them and mix with both kinds of flour to get a pliable dough.

3. Add water to the pounded pandan leaves and strain to extract juice. Add pandan juice to sweet potato dough get a good green colour and flavour.

4. Roll dough out into a long thin roll about 2.5-cm in diameter and cut it into pieces the size of small marbles. Shape each piece into a cup and put some of the sugar mixture into the hollow. Draw the dough together to close and shape into a neat ball.

5. Cook balls of dough in boiling water until they float. Drain well and toss them in grated coconut. Serve in banana-leaf boats.

Banana Pancakes

Preparation time 15 min • *Cooking time* 20–30 min

Plain flour 1 cup
Baking powder 1 tsp
Eggs 2, beaten
Milk ¹/₂ cup
Bananas (*pisang rajah*) 6, large and ripe
Castor sugar 1¹/₂ Tbsp
A pinch of salt
Cooking oil 1 Tbsp
Icing sugar 2 Tbsp
Lemon 1

1. Sieve plain flour and baking powder into a bowl. Make a well in the centre, add the eggs and half of the milk, mix well, and beat batter for 10 minutes until it is smooth and light. Add the remaining milk.

2. Peel and mash bananas together with castor sugar and salt. Mix mashed bananas with the batter.

3. Grease a frying pan, heat it and fry pancakes until they are brown on both sides. Grease the pan before frying another pancake.

4. Sprinkle a little icing sugar onto greaseproof paper and turn pancakes out onto it. Sprinkle each pancake with a little icing sugar and a squeeze of lemon juice. Fold into quarters and serve hot.

Jemput Pisang
(Banana Fritters)

Preparation time 10 min • *Cooking time* 10–15 min

Bananas (*pisang emas*) 300 g
Sugar 1¹/₂ Tbsp
Plain flour 3 heaped Tbsp, sifted
Cooking oil for deep-frying

1. Peel and mash bananas and mix thoroughly with sugar and plain flour. The dough should have a dropping consistency.

2. Heat cooking oil for deep-frying. When the oil is smoking hot, drop a tablespoonful of the mixture in one at a time and fry over medium heat until the banana fritters float and are a dark-brown colour. Try two or three first. If they are too soft for your taste, add a little more plain flour into the dough.

3. Drain well before serving.

Note: For best results, use really ripe bananas. If bananas are very sweet, use less sugar.

Vadai

Preparation time 30 min • *Cooking time* 20 min

Split black peas 300 g
Onion 1
Green chillies 3
Curry leaves 2 sprigs
Salt 1 tsp
A shake of pepper
Banana leaf 1, about a 10-cm square
Cooking oil for deep-frying

1. Wash and soak split peas for at least 4 hours, then grind or blend to a paste in an electric blender.

2. Dice the onion and chillies very finely. Shred the curry leaves very thinly.

3. Mix all the ingredients together with salt and pepper to taste. The mixture should be as soft as one can handle. Spread the banana leaf on a working surface. Brush it with cooking oil. Place a tablespoonful of the mixture on the oily leaf and shape it into a ring. With a quick twist of the wrist, turn the leaf over so that the ring slips gently from the oily leaf into a pan of hot oil. Fry until brown and well cooked. Drain well before serving.

Note: Any smooth, flat and oiled surface can take the place of the oiled banana leaf. If desired, a few unshelled shrimps can be pressed into the surface of each ring for added flavour.

Yam Puffs

Yam Puffs

Preparation time 1 hr • *Cooking time* 25 min • *Makes* 12

Cooking oil for deep-frying

PASTRY
Yam with head 300 g
Plain flour 30 g
Margarine 30 g, cold
Baking powder $^1/_4$ tsp
Ammonia bicarbonate $^1/_4$ tsp
Sesame oil $^1/_2$ tsp
A pinch of pepper
Sugar 1 tsp
Salt $^1/_2$ tsp

FILLING
Prawns 200 g
Pork or chicken meat 160 g
BBQ pork (*char siew*) (optional) 80 g
Cooking oil 1Tbsp
Sesame oil $^1/_2$ tsp
A pinch of pepper
Sugar 1 tsp
Salt $^1/_2$ tsp
Water $^1/_4$ cup
Cornflour 1 tsp, blended with 1 tsp water
Egg $^1/_2$, beaten

1. Make the pastry dough: slice yam thinly and steam until soft. Mash until fine while still warm. Add other ingredients listed under 'Pastry' and knead until dough is smooth. Keep dough covered until required.

2. Prepare the filling: shell prawns and wash them in salt water. Dice prawns, meat and BBQ pork.

3. Heat cooking oil and fry meat until it changes colour. Add sesame oil, pepper, sugar and salt, and finally add prawns and BBQ pork. Add water and fry until filling is cooked and water is absorbed. Add cornflour mixture to the filling. Remove pan from heat, pour beaten egg over the ingredients and stir quickly to mix and cook the egg. Cool filling on a plate.

4. Fry the puff: divide the pastry and filling into 12 portions. Wrap a portion of filling in each piece of pastry and shape into a neat puff. Dust fingers with flour if necessary while working.

5. Fry yam puffs in hot oil over a medium heat until they are brown and puffed up. Drain well and serve.

Curry Puffs

Preparation time 50–60 min • *Cooking time* 25–30 min

Cooking oil for deep-frying

FILLING
Lean meat 75 g of any type
Potato 1
Shallots 2
Curry powder 1 level Tbsp
Cooking oil 1 Tbsp
Curry leaves 4
Salt to taste
Water $^1/_2$ cup

PASTRY
Plain flour 1$^1/_2$ cups
Salt $^1/_4$ tsp
Margarine 5 Tbsp, cold
Cold water about 3 Tbsp

1. Prepare the filling: mince the meat. Peel and dice potato and chop shallots. Mix curry powder with a little water to get a paste.

2. Heat cooking oil and brown chopped shallots. Add curry leaves and curry paste and fry for 2–3 minutes. Add minced meat and fry for another 2–3 minutes. Add potato, salt and water. Cover and cook until potato is soft and filling dry, about 10 minutes. Season and cool filling thoroughly.

3. Make the pastry: sieve plain flour and salt into a bowl. Cut margarine into flour until it is in small pieces. With fingertips, rub margarine into flour very quickly until it resembles breadcrumbs. Add cold water to bind pastry. Turn the pastry onto a floured board and roll it out to 0.25-cm thickness. Cut it into rounds with a 5-cm round pastry cutter.

4. Put an equal amount of filling on each round of pastry, wet the edges of pastry rounds and fold over to make curry puffs. Press the edges together and twist the edge to seal.

5. Deep-fry curry puffs slowly in lightly smoking cooking oil until pastry is thoroughly cooked. Drain well and serve.

Yam Cake

Preparation time 40 min • *Cooking time* 40 min

Preserved Chinese radish
  (*tai tow choy*) 1 slice
Cooking oil 3 Tbsp
Shallots 2, sliced
Minced meat $^1/_2$ cup
Dried prawns 2 Tbsp, pounded
Chinese sausage (optional) 1, chopped
Yam 300 g, skinned and diced into
  1-cm cubes
Five spice powder (*ng heong fun*)
  $^1/_4$ tsp
Salt 1 tsp
Pepper $^1/_4$ tsp
Rice flour $^3/_4$ cup
Tapioca flour 2 Tbsp
Alkali water (*kan shui*) 1 tsp
Peanuts 2 Tbsp, roasted and crushed
Gingelly seeds $^1/_2$–1 Tbsp
Spring onion 1, diced

1. Soak preserved radish for at least 30 minutes. Heat cooking oil and brown the shallots. Add minced meat, dried prawns, Chinese sausage and preserved radish. Stir-fry together for 1 minute. Add yam cubes, five spice powder, salt and pepper and fry together for 3–4 minutes to lightly cook the yam.

2. Dish out the ingredients into a 20-cm steaming tray.

3. Sieve rice and tapioca flours together and knead them with alkali water and enough water to get $2^1/_2$ cups batter.

4. Heat up the steaming tray with the fried ingredients in it, pour in the batter and stir the mixture until it begins to thicken. Cover and steam for 30 minutes.

5. Remove the Yam Cake from the steamer, sprinkle peanuts, gingelly seeds and spring onion on top. Cool thoroughly before cutting into neat pieces. Serve with chilli sauce.

Note: Cold left-over Yam Cake can be sliced into 1-cm thick pieces and fried in a lightly greased pan until brown on both sides. It is delicious if served hot with chilli sauce. To crush fried peanuts, put peanuts in a plastic bag and crush with a rolling pin or a round cordial bottle.

Rampa Udang

(Glutinous Rice Rolls with Prawn Filling)

Preparation time $1^1/_2$ hr • *Cooking time* 50 min

Coconut $^3/_4$, grated
Lesser galangal (*cekur* or *sar keong*)
  1 piece
Shallots 5
Garlic 1 clove
Candlenuts (*buah keras*) 3
Peppercorns 6
Coriander seeds 1 Tbsp, roasted
Prawns $^1/_2$ cup, shelled
Cooking oil 2 Tbsp
Salt 1 tsp
Sugar $^1/_2$ tsp
Glutinous rice 300 g, soaked for 4 hours
Pandan (screwpine) leaves 2
Banana leaves 12 pieces, cut into 15-cm squares

1. In a dry pan, fry half portion of the grated coconut until evenly browned. Grind browned coconut until fine.

2. Grind lesser galangal, shallots, garlic, candlenuts, peppercorns and roasted coriander seeds until fine. Shell and dice the prawns.

3. Heat cooking oil and fry ground spices for 3–4 minutes. Add prawns, ½ tsp salt and sugar and fry until prawns are well cooked. Finally, add ground fried coconut and mix well. Season to taste and set aside to cool.

4. Drain glutinous rice. Put it with $^1/_2$ tsp salt and pandan leaves, shredded lengthwise and tied into a knot, in a steaming tray and steam for 15 minutes.

5. Extract $^1/_4$ cup coconut milk from the remaining grated coconut. After rice has been steamed for 15 minutes, turn it out into the coconut milk, mix well, and return rice to the steaming tray to steam for another 10 minutes until well cooked.

6. Scald the pieces of banana leaf to soften. Divide rice and filling into 12 equal portions each. Spread one portion of rice lengthwise in the centre of one banana leaf square. Put filling on it and fold the rice over to shape it into a roll of about 5-cm long and 2.5-cm wide. Wrap each roll firmly in a piece of banana leaf, press the ends together and staple to secure. Trim away excess lengths of leaf and place wrapped rolls into a hot, dry frying pan to brown leaves all over. Turn rolls to get them evenly browned.

Rampa Udang (Glutinous Rice Rolls with Prawn Filling)

Miscellaneous Favourites

Simple Fritter Batter

Preparation time 5 min

Plain flour 4 Tbsp
Cornflour 2 Tbsp
Baking powder $1/2$ tsp
Water 5 Tbsp
Salt $1/2$ tsp
Cooking oil 1 tsp

1. Mix the dry ingredients together in a bowl and make a well in the centre. Add three quarters the measured amount of water into the well and stir quickly to get a thick batter. Add the rest of the water as batter thickens.

2. Add cooking oil and mix until batter is smooth. If batter is too thick, add more water. Use immediately to coat food for frying.

Note: This batter is easy to make and is light and crisp. It is suitable for both sweet and savoury fritters such as prawn fritters, banana fritters and sweet potato fritters.

Soy Bean Milk

Preparation time 20 min • Cooking time 10-15 min

Soy beans 150 g, soaked for 4 hours
Water 6 cups
Granulated sugar $3/4$ cup
Ginger 2 slices
Pandan (screwpine) leaves 2

1. Put soaked soy beans with 2 cups water in a blender. Blend at high speed until a smooth pulp is obtained. Pour pulp into a calico bag and squeeze it through 4 cups of water. Squeeze pulp until it is really dry.

2. Pour soy bean milk into a saucepan, add pandan leaves and ginger slices and bring to a boil. When it boils, add sugar. As soon as it boils again, remove the pan from heat.

3. Soy bean milk can be served hot or cold. When chilled, it is a very refreshing drink.

Roti Jala

(Lacy Pancake)

Preparation time 15 min • Cooking time 20–25 min

Coconut $1/2$, grated
Plain flour 1 cup
Salt $1/2$ tsp
Egg 1, beaten
Pandan (screwpine) leaves 2
Cooking oil 1 Tbsp

1. Extract 1 cup coconut milk from the grated coconut. Sift plain flour and salt into a mixing bowl. Make a well in the centre and drop in the egg and half the coconut milk.

2. With a wooden spoon, stir egg and coconut milk into the flour to get a smooth batter. Add more coconut milk if necessary. Beat the batter for about 10 minutes until it is smooth and bubbly.

3. Mix the rest of the coconut milk into the batter, cover the bowl with a tea towel and leave the batter to stand for 20 minutes.

4. Fold pandan leaves and tie them together to get a 15-cm brush. If pandan leaves are not available, tie a piece of clean muslin to the end of a stick.

5. Heat a frying pan and grease it by brushing with the pandan or muslin brush dipped in oil.

6. Pour some batter into a Roti Jala mould and, moving it in a circular motion, let it drop to form a thin, lacy pancake in the hot frying pan. When it is cooked, fold it into quarters and transfer to a plate. Cover with a clean tea towel to keep it moist and warm. Continue making Roti Jala, one at a time, until all the batter is used up.

7. Stack Roti Jala neatly on a plate and serve with Chicken Curry (page 44).

Roti Jala (Lacy Pancake)

 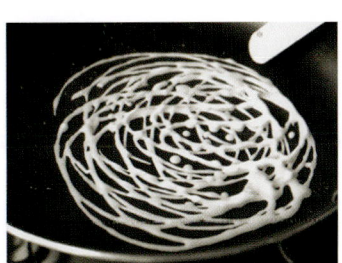 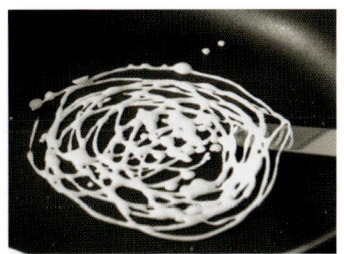 

Poh Piah

Preparation time 1–1 1/2 hr • Cooking time 40–50 min • Makes 24 rolls

Poh piah skin 24 sheets
Hoisin sauce (*teem cheong*) 1/2 cup

GARNISH
Eggs 2
Salt 1/4 tsp
A shake of pepper
Chinese sausages (optional) 1 pair
Garlic 10 cloves, finely chopped
Cooking oil 6 Tbsp
Shallots 20, sliced
Firm bean curd (*pak towfoo*) 2 pieces,
    shredded
Bean sprouts 1 cup, tailed
Cucumber 1/2
Lettuce 1 head
Coriander leaves 1 sprig
Red chillies 15

FILLING
Prawns 300 g
Salt 2 tsp
Sugar 1/2 tsp
Pork or chicken 300 g
Yam bean (*bangkuang*) 900 g
French beans 10
Cooking oil 2 Tbsp
Crabmeat 1/2 cup
Light soy sauce 2 tsp

PREPARE THE GARNISH

1. Beat eggs with salt and a good shake of pepper. Heat and lightly grease a frying pan. Make three very thin omelettes. Roll each omelette into a tight roll and shred very finely. Loosen and pile shredded omelette onto small dish.

2. Fry sausages (optional) until evenly browned. Slice them thinly and put them onto another small dish.

3. Fry chopped garlic in 2 Tbsp cooking oil until evenly browned. Remove browned garlic and oil to a small dish.

4. Heat another 2 Tbsp cooking oil and brown sliced shallots. Drain browned shallots and remove them to another small dish.

5. Fry bean curd shreds until firm, drain well and remove to a small dish.

6. Blanch the bean sprouts. Cut cucumber into 0.8-cm fingers. Wash and dry lettuce leaves and coriander leaves. Halve each lettuce leaf along the central vein. Arrange the vegetables neatly on a flat dish. Pound chillies to a fine paste and remove this to a small dish.

PREPARE THE FILLING

7. Clean, dice and season prawns with 1/2 tsp salt and 1/2 tsp sugar. Clean, parboil and shred pork or chicken finely. Shred yam bean and French beans.

8. Toss shredded French beans in the remaining hot cooking oil to cook them lightly. Set aside. Fry shredded parboiled meat in the same oil until meat is cooked, then add light soy sauce and prawns . Stir-fry for a minute. Add yam bean and 1 1/2 tsp salt and stir-fry until yam bean is cooked and a little tender. This should take about 15 minutes. Now mix in the French beans, crabmeat then season to taste and keep hot until required.

TO SERVE

9. The poh piah skins should be piled on a plate and covered with damp muslin to keep them from drying out. The hot meat filling is placed in a deep dish surrounded by the garnishes attractively arranged in small dishes around it.

10. To make the Poh Piah, place a skin on a plate, put a piece of lettuce leaf on it and spread a thin layer of prepared chilli sauce and hoisin sauce on the lettuce. Place a little of each garnish on top of the lettuce and finally spread 1 Tbsp of the hot filling on top of everything. Fold in the sides first, then one of the other edges. Tuck in firmly and roll up. Poh Piah should be eaten immediately as the skin becomes soggy after a while.

Kuih Pietee

(Top Hats)

Preparation time 20 min • *Cooking time* 40–50 min

Plain flour 4 Tbsp
Rice flour $^3/_4$ cup
Salt $^1/_4$ tsp
Egg 1, beaten
Coconut milk or water $^3/_4$ cup
Cooking oil for deep-frying
Coriander leaves 1 sprig, plucked

1. Sift both kinds of flour and salt into a mixing bowl. Make a well in the centre, add the egg and liquid (coconut milk or water) and mix to get a smooth batter. Beat batter for 10 minutes until it is bubbly. Cover batter and let it rest for 20 minutes.

2. Heat a saucepan two-third full of cooking oil for deep-frying. Heat the Pietee mould in hot oil.

3. When the mould is well heated and oil is smoking hot, lift it out and give it a gentle shake to remove excess oil before dipping it in batter. The batter should just reach the top of the mould.

4. Immerse batter-covered mould in hot oil. When the cup is brown, a gentle shake loosens it from the mould. Lift cups up with a perforated spoon and drain them well. Cool and store in airtight containers.

5. It might take 5–10 spoilt hats before the mould becomes 'seasoned,' but when this happens and the oil is at the correct temperature, the cups can be made very quickly.

6. To serve, fill cups with Poh Piah filling (refer to page 156). Garnish with coriander leaves and chilli sauce.

Steamboat

Preparation time 1–1½ hr • Serves 4–6

Chicken meat 225 g
Fillet steak 225 g
Light soy sauce for marinade 1 tsp
Sesame oil 1 tsp
Cornflour 2 tsp
Pig's liver 225 g
Threadfin (*ikan kurau*) 225 g, cleaned
   and sliced
Salt 1 tsp
Ginger 2.5-cm knob, juice extracted
Prawns 8–12, large
Sugar 1 tsp
Soft bean curd (*towfoo*) 2 pieces
Lettuce 225 g
Spinach 225 g
Chinese cabbage 225 g
Rice vermicelli or transparent
noodles 120 g
Chilli sauce ¹/₂ cup
Light soy sauce for dipping 1 Tbsp
   per person
Cooking oil ¹/₂ cup
A large saucepan of chicken and/or
   pork stock
Egg 1 per person

1. Slice chicken and steak as thinly as possible and marinate chicken and steak in light soy sauce, sesame oil and 1 tsp cornflour.

2. Slice liver and fish to 0.25-cm thickness and marinate liver in ¹/₂ tsp salt, 1 tsp cornflour and ginger juice.

3. Clean prawns and remove shell between head and tail. Slit back of prawns and devein them. Season in 1 tsp sugar and the remaining salt.

4. Cut each piece of bean curd into 4 pieces. Cut lettuce, spinach and cabbage into 5-cm lengths.

5. Soak rice vermicelli or transparent noodles in water until soft. Drain well and remove to a dish.

6. Lay each type of vegetable on a flat plate and arrange one type of sliced meat on each bed of vegetables. Prawns, sliced fish and bean curd can be arranged on one plate. Chilli sauce, soy sauce and oil should be ladled out into several small saucers and placed conveniently around the table.

7. The steamboat pot is placed at the centre of the table, with the dishes of vegetable and meat arranged around it. The stock should be boiling in the pot at the start of the meal and should be maintained at a gentle boil throughout, with more stock added from time to time and whenever necessary.

8. Each diner has a small dish and a bowl in front of him. He may beat the egg immediately in the bowl with a teaspoon of light soy sauce for dipping or leave the egg until the end of the meal. Using a pair of chopsticks or a long wire ladle, each person selects some meat and vegetable and dips it into the section of the pot directly in front of him. When cooking vegetables in the stock, he should spoon a little oil over the vegetables. The cooked food may be dipped into the beaten egg to lightly cool it so that it is the right temperature for eating. It can also be dipped in chilli sauce or soy sauce.

9. The diner who wishes to have some rice vermicelli or transparent noodles to go with the food will put a little rice vermicelli or transparent noodles into his bowl (either over any egg that is left or without the egg) and soup is ladled over the vermicelli or noodles.

Note: As an alternative to a steamboat pot, an electric rice cooker may be used.

Cooking
Tips

Cooking Terms

BARBECUE

Barbecuing food involves cooking it over hot charcoal or on a revolving spit.

BASTE

To baste food, spoon melted fat, food juices or other liquid (such as marinade) over meat during cooking to keep the meat moist and to improve the flavour.

BLANCH

Some recipes require blanching meat, which means to plunge it into boiling water to loosen the skin, remove strong flavours, deactivate enzymes or to partially pre-cook it.

BLEND

When food such as a starch or any ground cereal is mixed with a liquid to be blended, a smooth purée is achieved.

BRAISE

Braised food, such as meat, is cooked in a covered pan and cooked in a small quantity of liquid at very low temperature until it is tender. Braised foods have a better flavour if they are first browned in some fat.

CHOP

To chop is to cut into very small pieces. Use a longish knife with a pointed blade, such as a cook's knife. Hold the knife in your dominant hand and using your other hand, grasp the pointed end of the blade between the thumb and fingers. Hold the pointed end stationary while the blade is moved up and down quickly on the food to chop it.

COAT

In order for food to be fried completely and evenly, it is important to coating it with a thin layer of beaten egg or batter, or with a dry substance like flour or bread-crumbs, as this prevents food from breaking up and keeps it tender and moist.

DICE

Food that is diced is cut into even-sized cubes. First, cut food into slices, then strips and finally cut across the strips to get cubes.

FILLET

A fillet is a boneless strip of lean meat or the deboned sides of a fish.

FRY

a. Dry-frying refers to frying foods such as peanuts, gingelly seeds or grated coconut in a hot frying pan without any cooking oil. The food is stirred continuously to prevent burning until it is browned and cooked.

b. Stir-frying or sautéing refers to tossing food in a hot frying pan with only enough cooking oil to lightly coat the pan to prevent sticking.

c. Deep-frying refers to cooking food immersed in hot oil. The cooking oil should be very hot when the food is put in so that the coating is cooked immediately to seal in the juices. After the food has been put in, turn down the heat to enable the food to cook slowly without burning.

GARNISH

Garnishes add a decorative touch to a dish, and they should be edible. Garnishes include parsley, spring onions, coriander leaves, chillies, tomatoes, hard-boiled eggs and lemon.

GULAI

This is a Malay word used extensively in Penang, Johor and Melaka to refer to a type of curry.

KERABU

Kerabu is a spicy salad that is made from either dried or fresh prawns.

LAKSA

This is a dish of noodles with a spicy soup that is made with fish or prawns.

MARINADE

A marinade refers to sauces and seasoning used to flavour and to tenderise meat or fish before cooking.

PEDAS

This is a Malay word that means hot, like the taste of chillies.

SCALD

Scalding has different meanings. Milk is scalded by bringing it to boiling point in order to retard souring. Meats can also be scalded by pouring boiling water over them to remove the skin, and to loosen hairs or feathers. In general, food can sometimes be scalded as part of a cleaning process.

Cutting Methods

SHRED

To shred is to cut or grate into long, thin strips.

SIMMER

To simmer is to cook food in liquid below boiling point. The liquid around the food should be just lightly moving or shivering, and not bubbling. When simmering, there is no evaporation of liquid.

SKIM

To skim is to remove fat or scum from the surface of a liquid. This is done by drawing a metal spoon across the surface.

STEAM

To steam is to cook food over boiling water.

STEW

Stewing refers to slow cooking in a seasoned liquid kept at simmering point. The liquid is thickened and served with the food as gravy.

STOCK

A stock is a well flavoured liquid made by simmering bones and bits of meat for at least an hour. Strain the liquid to remove bones and skim off all fat before using it as the base for soups or gravy.

SAMBAL

Sambal is a spicy mixture of chillies pounded or ground with dried shrimp paste (*belacan*) or other spices.

SAMBAL BELACAN (SPICY SHRIMP PASTE)

This can be made by pounding resh chillies with roasted dried shrimp paste (*belacan*): Proportion: 3–4 chillies to a 2.5 x 2.5 x 0.5-cm piece dried shrimp paste. Cut the chillies into 1-cm pieces and pound together with the roasted dried shrimp paste just enough to mix the ingredients; the chillies should not be too finely pounded. A couple of lime leaves can be pounded with this mixture if desired. Squeeze some lime juice over the sambal just before serving.

TUMIS

This is a Malay word, which means to stir-fry in cooking oil to cook and improve flavour, e.g. *tumis sambal* before adding liquid and other ingredients to it.

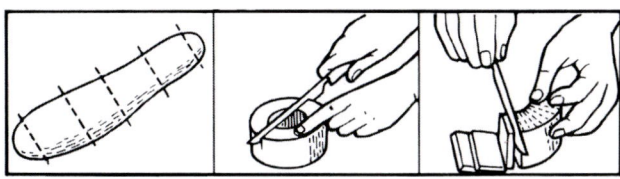

For acar

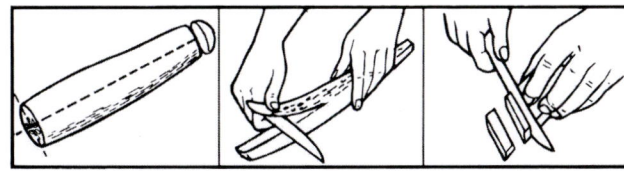

For kerabu

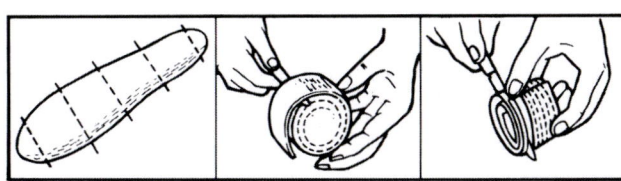

Curls for garnishing

Cooking Hints

1. Meats can be cleaned and prepared ready for use. They can be minced, sliced or cut up as required, packed into plastic boxes in portions sufficient for a meal, labelled and kept in the freezer until required.

2. Prawns and fish can also be shelled, cleaned and cut up as required before packing and putting in the freezer to freeze for 2–3 weeks until required.

3. Grated coconut can be stored in the freezer. Take it out at least 1 hour before it is required to give it time to thaw.

4. Ground curry or sambal ingredients, including *sambal belacan* (spicy shrimp paste), can be prepared in bulk and stored in the freezer to be used as required. For sambal belacan, it is better to freeze it without the lime juice, which can be added just before serving.

5. Shallots and garlic can be chopped or sliced in advance, kept in plastic boxes with tight-fitting lids to keep the smell in, and stored in the fridge for use during the week.

6. To fry crispy brown shallots, make sure the shallots are sliced evenly to ensure even cooking. For 1 cup sliced shallots, heat up about 1 cup cooking oil in a frying pan. When the oil is smoking hot, add in the shallots and stir them around in the hot oil until they are just beginning to brown. Turn down the heat and continue stirring until the shallots are a light golden-brown. Remove them from the oil with a draining spoon, drain them on kitchen paper and when they are cool, store them in an airtight jar.

7. To fry browned garlic, chop the skinned garlic until very fine. For 1 Tbsp chopped garlic, heat up 1 Tbsp cooking oil in a frying pan. When the oil is hot, add the prepared garlic and stir in the hot oil till it begins to brown around the sides. Turn off the heat altogether or remove the pan from the fire and continue stirring the garlic in the oil until evenly browned. Collect the browned garlic to one side of the pan and scoop them up into a dish to cool. When cool, store them in an airtight jar with or without the oil, as desired.

8. To roast peanuts, rub peanuts in a tea towel or between two sheets of kitchen tissue to remove dust and dirt. Put the peanuts into a wok or a frying pan and dry-fry over low heat for 20–25 minutes, stirring all the time until the peanuts are evenly browned and cooked. Turn the browned peanuts into a colander, and with the help of a pair of cotton gloves to protect the fingers from getting burnt, rub the peanuts against the colander to remove the skin. Shake the colander and the skin can be blown away quite easily. When the peanuts are cool, store in an airtight container.

9. To grind peanuts—the electric blender does this very quickly. To prevent peanuts getting too finely ground, switch on the blender and off immediately and you will get coarsely ground peanuts and not powdered peanuts.

10. To grind curry ingredients and *sambal*—the electric blender does this quickly too. Cut up the ingredients roughly before putting them in the blender. Candlenut needs thin slicing before it will blend well. Add water as instructed in the recipe and blend the ingredients to the fineness required. Always remember that blended sambals require a longer time to fry (*tumis*) so that the water in the sambal will be evaporated.

11. To fry or *tumis* curry or sambal ingredients—heat up 5–6 Tbsp cooking oil for every cup of ground ingredients. Fry the ground ingredients in the hot oil with $1/2$ tsp salt over a low fire, stirring all the time for 5–10 minutes until the oil seems to separate from the ground ingredients. This is the stage when curry or sambal ingredients are said to be cooked and aromatic.

12. To prepare and clean prawns:

a. Shell prawns, slit them down the back and devein them. Mix 1 Tbsp salt with each pound of prawns and leave them for 10 minutes. Wash them well and drain them. Either use them immediately or pack them in portions and freeze them at once.

b. When prawns are to be cooked with their shells, cut off part of the head from where the beak begins. With the help of the sharp beak just cut off, dig into the cut head, just under the shell, and remove the gritty sac. Trim off the legs and rub the prawns all over with salt. After 10 minutes, wash away the salt, drain the prawns and they are ready for cooking or freezing.

c. Freshwater prawns should have part of the head from where the beak begins cut off. When this is done, split each prawn in two lengthwise. Remove the gritty sac in the head and the vein along the back. Wash the prawns, drain well before seasoning them for cooking. Freshwater prawns should be eaten as fresh as possible and should not be kept for more than 3 days in the freezer.

13. To use curry powder. Always blend curry powder into a paste with water before you fry or *tumis* it.

14. To make special salt, fry together salt and five spice powder for several minutes.

15. Cooking Rice (For 1 cup of rice, use 1 cup water)

With the electric rice cooker, boiling rice has become a very simple matter. One has only to follow the instructions that come with the rice cooker and fluffy rice is the result. However, cooking rice without a rice cooker is just as easy. Here are a few points to remember. The secret lies in the correct amount of water added to the rice before boiling and in the very slow cooking for the last 15 minutes after the water has been absorbed. The amount of water needed depends partly on the type of rice used, so get to know the rice you use. After washing the rice, drain away the water and add in the measured amount of water. Cover the pan and allow the rice to cook until all the water is absorbed. If the rice looks uncooked at this stage, it needs more water, so add ¼–½ cup more water and allow it to cook again until the water is absorbed. When the water is absorbed, the rice grains have all burst but they do not look fluffy. It is then necessary to turn the fire down to as low as possible, or if an electric hot plate is being used, turn it off. Keep the pan covered and allow the rice to finish cooking and dry out for the last 15 minutes. When dishing up rice for serving, loosen the rice first with a shallow rice ladle so that the rice becomes loose, fluffy grains.

16. Pandan (Screwpine) Juice

This is a basic ingredient for many Malaysian dishes and it is not always readily available. Although pandan essence can be used as a substitute, it is not available in some countries. Moreover, the essence, while giving the flavour, does not give the colour and so artificial colouring has to be used. If pandan leaves are available, they should be used, as their flavour and colour cannot be matched by any artificial flavours and colours. To get pandan juice, wash 10–12 pandan leaves (the older ones are better), pile about 5–6 leaves together and pound them until they are all fibrous-looking. Wrap the pounded pandan leaves in a damp piece of calico and squeeze out the juice. This pandan juice colours the food and at the same time gives it the lovely pandan flavour.

17. Extracting Coconut Milk

The easiest method to extract coconut milk is to use a calico bag. Coconut milk can be extracted from the grated flesh of mature fresh coconuts. Grated coconut is sold in the wet markets, but to do it yourself, gently knock the shell of a mature nut all over with the back of a heavy chopper or axe. This helps to loosen the flesh from the hard shell. Then with a hard knock, crack the nut in half and either pry the flesh from the shell with a sharp knife or chop away small pieces of the shell until all is removed. Peel away the brown skin from the white flesh, wash them and then grate them with a coarse grater.

To extract coconut milk, have 2 bowls ready, one of about 2 cups capacity and the other of about 4 cups capacity. Fill the larger bowl with 2 cups water. Fill the rinsed calico bag with about ¼ grated coconut and squeeze out as much thick milk as possible into the small bowl. Then place the whole bag of coconut into the second bowl and knead the bag of grated coconut in the water to get the second milk. Squeeze the bag of grated coconut as dry as possible before throwing the contents away. Repeat with the next lot of grated coconut and continue until coconut milk has been extracted from all the grated coconut. When emptying the grated coconut from the bag, turn the whole bag inside out so that the coconut fibres do not stick to the outside of the bag. Then turn the whole bag back the right way again before filling it with grated coconut once more. In this way it is possible to get ¾–1 cup thick milk from one grated coconut.

Grated coconut can be frozen and kept until required. To extract milk from frozen grated coconut, place it in an electric blender with 2 cups hot water and blend for 30 seconds. Pour portions of the blended mixture into a rinsed calico bag and squeeze out as much milk as possible.

Desiccated coconut from a tin can be soaked in 3 cups hot water for at least 15 minutes, or until mixture cools.

Instant and frozen coconut cream and tinned coconut cream are readily available from supermarkets.

Glossary

PANDAN (SCREWPINE) LEAVES
Daun Pandan (M)

Lim Pei Yip (C)

A member of the pandanus or screwpine family, these stiff and long blades of leaves with a pronounced furrow down its centre are used to give a distinctive flavour to many dishes throughout Southeast Asia. The leaves may be added when cooking rice or desserts for added fragrance. They may also be pounded and the green juice extracted to be added to food for colouring in addition to flavouring. The leaves are sometimes also used to wrap around morsels of food before frying or grilling, or fashioned into containers for desserts.

ANGLED LOOFAH
Ketola (M)

See Kua (C)

A dark green gourd about 25–30 cm long with hard, angular ridges running down its whole length. The flesh is soft and white.

BITTER GOURD
Peria (M)

Fu Gua (C)

A wrinkled light green gourd, this vegetable has bitter-tasting flesh. It is used extensively in Southeast Asian cooking, in soups, salads and stir-fries.

LEMON GRASS
Serai (M)

Heong Mow (C)

A tall grass with very fleshy leaf bases that are used for flavouring food, especially curries. Use only 10–12 cm of the slightly swollen leaf bases. When sliced and dried, they keep very well. Fresh lemon grass is available from Chinese grocery stores.

SWEET POTATO GREENS
Farn Su Mew (C)

The young leaves and shoots of the sweet potato creeper, sweet potato greens are excellent sources of Vitamin A and Vitamin C. Peel off the tough fibrous skin from the stems before cooking. The leaves may be boiled or stir-fried.

CHINESE RADISH
Lobak (M)

Lopak (C)

A member of the mustard family, this long, white, cylindrical root measures 20–45 cm (8–18 in) long. Choose those that are firm when gently squeezed. The flesh should be crisp and juicy.

KAFFIR LIME LEAVES
Daun Limau Purut (M)

Fatt Foong Kum Yip (C)

These leaves are often pounded with sambal belacan (spicy shrimp paste) to give it a lemony flavour. The leaves can be shredded or added whole to flavour curries. Kaffir lime leaves keep well when sealed in a plastic bag and frozen. They retain their flavour when thawed. The fruit is favoured for its rind.

POLYGONUM LEAVES
Daun Kesum (M)

Also known as laksa leaves, this plant rarely grows taller than 25 cm. The thin, narrow and pointed leaves are about 4 cm long and 1 cm wide. They are commonly used to flavour laksa gravy and also eaten raw in Thai salads.

YAM BEAN
Bangkuang, Sengkuang (M)

Sar Gott (C)

This tuberous root has a brown skin that can be easily peeled away from the white flesh. The flesh is sweet and can be eaten raw or cooked.

Note: M = Malay C = Cantonese

Pandan (Screwpine) Leaves

Angled Loofah

Bitter Gourd

Lemon Grass

Sweet Potato Greens

Chinese Radish

Kaffir Lime Leaves

Polygonum Leaves

Yam Bean

CORIANDER LEAVES

Daun Ketumbar (M)

Yim Sai (C)

The young leaves of the coriander seedlings that is used much in the same way that parsley is. In fact, coriander leaves are sometimes called Chinese parsley. It is commonly used to flavour soups and broths and as a garnishing.

POINTED PEPPER LEAVES

Daun Kaduk (M)

Gar Lowe (C)

A shiny, club-shaped leaf from a weak-stemmed plant that grows wild in the tropics. It grows along the side of many roads and can be found growing as weeds in many gardens. Its peculiar flavour may not be acceptable to many people.

WATER CONVOLVULUS

Kangkung (M)

Ung Choy (C)

A green leafy vegetable that can be found growing wild beside streams. Some varieties have purple stems. If unavailable, substitute with spinach or watercress.

CHIVES

Kucai (M)

Kow Choy (C)

A small, onion-like plant with long, narrow, flat leaves. It is best eaten raw or very lightly cooked. The yellow variety, called kow wong in Chinese, is a vegetable that is much sought after.

SPRING ONION

Daun Bawang (M)

Choong (C)

The young onion with an immature bulb. The round, hallow leaves and unformed bulb of the spring onion has a mild flavour and is used as a vegetable, as a garnishing and for flavouring.

BAMBOO SHOOT

Rebung (M)

Choke So-Un (C)

The young shoot of the bamboo. Fresh bamboo shoot must be boiled for at least 1 hour to soften it before it can be used. After boiling, soak it in water till required. Boiled and ready-to-use bamboo shoot is available from Chinese grocery stores and some supermarkets.

TORCH GINGER BUD

Bunga Kantan (M)

Lam Keong Fah (C)

The pink flower buds of a variety of ginger that looks very similar to the galangal plant. It is used as a flavouring in many dishes, and especially in fish curries.

LESSER GALANGAL

Cekur (M)

Sar Keong (C)

A miniature member of the ginger family with leaves not more than 10 cm long and the rhizomes less than 2.5 cm long. It has a very pronounced aromatic flavour. It is available fresh from market stalls selling home produce. Chinese medicine shops sell the dried version which comes in round slices.

GALANGAL

Lengkuas (M)

Lam Keong (C)

A rhizome of the ginger family that is a very popular flavouring used in Malaysian cooking. It has a shiny off-white skin with brown markings. The white flesh is fairly hard and fibrous. It can be sliced, dried and stored for later use.

MUSTARD CABBAGE

Kai Choy (C)

This variety of mustard cabbage is distinguished by large gnarled stems and broad leaves. It is very popular in Asian cooking for pickling, soups or stir-fries. It has a mild flavor that increases in pungency as the plant matures. Some people do not like its pungency. Blanching in hot water may reduce the pungent flavour.

FLOWERING CABBAGE

Sayur Sawi (M)

Choy Sum (C)

Plants of about 30 cm tall with long, green, leafy stalks surmounted with round-bladed, dark green leaves. Also known as the flowering cabbage, these greens sprout yellow flowers at the shoot. The flowers are cooked along with the greens and stems. They are commonly boiled, stir-fried or steamed.

Note: M = Malay   C = Cantonese

Coriander Leaves

Pointed Pepper Leaves

Water Convolvulus

Chives

Spring Onion

Bamboo Shoot

Torch Ginger Bud

Lesser Galangal

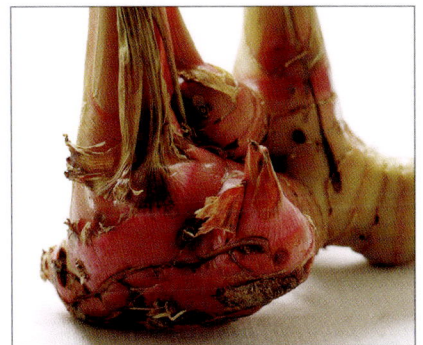

Galangal

Mustard Cabbage

Flowering Cabbage

PRESERVED SPINACH
Mui Choy (C)

Preserved in salt, this vegetable should be soaked and thoroughly washed before use to remove any grit and excess salt. It imparts an excellent flavour to foods and is most commonly used in steamed dishes with minced meats.

DRIED SOUR FRUIT SLICES
Asam Gelugur (M)
Asam Pei (C)

Dried sour fruit slices usually available from Chinese grocery stores. If not available, substitute with tamarind pulp.

PRESERVED RADISH
Choy Poh (C)

The cleaned and skinned radish is cut into even-sized pieces and is preserved with spices and salt to get golden brown pieces that are crisp and delicious eaten as a relish. There is also another type of preserved radish known in Chinese as tai tou choy. The latter is made from whole radish cut into slices lengthwise and with all the leaves intact, salted and dried.

SZECHUAN VEGETABLE
Char Choy (C)

The heart of the mustard cabbage preserved in salt and chilli, making it very salty and spicy. It is available in wet markets and Chinese grocery stores. Kept in an airtight container, it will keep for several months in the refrigerator.

PRESERVED CABBAGE
Tong Choy (C)

Available loose from Chinese grocery stores, these are squarish pieces of golden brown cabbage leaves preserved and packed into squat, round, glazed earthen jars.

PRESERVED SOY BEANS
Tow Cheong or Mien See (C)

Preserved soy beans are used to flavour food or to make flavourful sauces. The beans can be used whole or mashed to make a paste.

SZECHUAN PEPPER
Fah Chew (C)

Small, dried berries about the size of coriander seeds. They are reddish brown in colour and can be bought from Chinese medicine stores. They are now also available on the spice racks of supermarkets.

SESAME SEEDS
Zee Ma (C)

These tiny, flat seeds have a nutty flavour and a high oil content. They can be eaten raw or toasted. To toast sesame seeds, fry in a dry, hot pan until the seeds start to cackle and 'jump.' Stir them around constantly to prevent burning.

WONTON SKIN
Wonton Pei (C)

Paper-thin squares of egg noodle dough, about 7.5-cm wide. They are usually available wherever fresh egg noodle is sold. Keep covered as they dry out easily.

HOISIN SAUCE
Teem Cheong (C)

This is a very thick, sweet, red sauce made from soy beans, flour, sugar, spices and food colouring. It is used to marinate foods and is also used as a condiment at the table. Comes in bottles or tins and will keep for several months in the refrigerator.

POH PIAH SKIN
Poh Piah Pei (C)

A paper-thin pancake most commonly used to make spring rolls. It can be deep-fried or eaten as it is. Keep covered as they dry out easily.

Note: M = Malay   C = Cantonese

Preserved Spinach

Preserved Radish

Szechuan Vegetable

Dried Sour Fruit Slices

Preserved Cabbage

Preserved Soy Beans

Szechuan Pepper

Sesame Seeds

Wonton Skin

Hoisin Sauce

Poh Piah Skin

FIRM BEAN CURD
Pak Towfoo (C)

These firm bean curd squares are easier to handle than the soft variety, but the texture is not as smooth.

DRIED PRAWNS
Udang Kering (M)
Har Mai (C)

These are sun-dried salted, steamed prawns. Soak them in water for about 20 minutes to remove excess salt before using. Dried prawns are ground, chopped or left whole and fried to flavour dishes.

DRIED ANCHOVIES
Ikan Bilis (M)
Kon Yu Chai (C)

Remove the head and intestines, rinse quickly and dry thoroughly before storing. Keeps very well. Fry them in deep-fat when they are dry and they make delicious, crisp titbits for cocktails. They are available in wet markets and Chinese grocery stores.

SOFT BEAN CURD
Towfoo (C)

Soft bean curd is available in slabs from the wet market or in rectangular containers and tubes from the supermarket. It has the texture of baked custard. Handle carefully to prevent breaking it.

WOOD EAR FUNGUS
Mok Yee (C)

A dried fungus that thrives on rotting wood. This looks like elephant's ears and is black on the top and light brownish-white on the underside. Soak in warm water for about 20 minutes before using. It is available from Chinese grocery stores and supermarkets and will keep indefinitely, stored in cool, dry conditions.

CANDLENUTS
Buah Keras (M)
Saik Ki Chai (C)

The oily kernel of a round nut, about 3 cm in diameter, with a very hard furrowed shell. The kernel looks very much like the macadamia nut and is used to thicken and enrich curries. If unavailable, use Brazil nuts or macadamia nuts as a substitute.

DRIED BEAN CURD SKIN

Dried bean curd skin can be found in stick (*fu chok*) or sheet (*fu pei*) form. Dried bean curd skins are thin, yellow pieces of skin formed on the top of soy bean milk before it coagulates. *Fu chok* is commonly used in desserts. *Fu pei* comes in sheets about 60 cm wide. They are sold folded like plastic sheets and are available at stores selling bean curd, Chinese grocery stores and supermarkets.

HARD BEAN CURD SLICES
Teem Chok (C)

Seasoned, brown rectangular pieces of dried soy bean curd. These are used mainly in vegetarian cooking.

PALM SUGAR
Gula Melaka (M)
Yea Tong (C)

Cakes of dark brown sugar made from the sap of the coconut palm. Good quality palm sugar has a very strong flavour of coconut.

SAGO
Sar Kok Mai (C)

In this book, we use pearl sago which is manufactured from sago flour obtained from the pith of the sago palm. Sago is available in different sizes from supermarkets.

AGAR-AGAR STRIPS
Lam Keon (C)

A seaweed used widely in Southeast Asia for making jellies. It has better setting qualities than gelatine and can set without refrigeration. It is available in strips or powder form from Chinese grocery stores or supermarkets.

Note: M = Malay   C = Cantonese

Firm White Bean Curd

Dried Prawns

Dried Anchovies

Soft Bean Curd

Wood Ear Fungus

Candlenuts

Dried Bean Curd Stick

Dried Bean Curd Skin

Hard Bean Curd Slices

Palm Sugar

Sago

Agar-Agar Strips

Weights and Measures

Accuracy in measuring and weighing ingredients is essential for successful cooking, particularly so with light desserts and cakes where incorrect amounts of ingredients could spoil the dish altogether.

The measures used in this cookbook are in Metric and the American standard measuring cups and spoons. The measuring cups are easily obtainable in sets of four—1 cup, $^1/_2$ cup, $^1/_3$ cup and $^1/_4$ cup. The cup is equivalent to 8 ounces. The spoons are also easily available in sets of four—1 Tbsp, 1 tsp, $^1/_2$ tsp and $^1/_4$ tsp.

It must be remembered that when measuring dry ingredients, always fill the measure to overflowing and without shaking it, level off with the straight edge of a knife, unless otherwise specified in the recipe.

LIQUID AND VOLUME MEASURES

Metric	Imperial	American
5 ml	$^1/_6$ fl oz	1 tsp
10 ml	$^1/_3$ fl oz	1 dsp
15 ml	$^1/_2$ fl oz	1 Tbsp
60 ml	2 fl oz	$^1/_4$ cup (4 Tbsp)
85 ml	2 $^1/_2$ fl oz	$^1/_3$ cup
90 ml	3 fl oz	$^3/_8$ cup (6 Tbsp)
125 ml	4 fl oz	$^1/_2$ cup
180 ml	6 fl oz	$^3/_4$ cup
250 ml	8 fl oz	1 cup
300 ml	10 fl oz ($^1/_2$ pint)	1 $^1/_4$ cups
375 ml	12 fl oz	1 $^1/_2$ cups
435 ml	14 fl oz	1 $^3/_4$ cups
500 ml	16 fl oz	2 cups
625 ml	20 fl oz (1 pint)	2 $^1/_2$ cups
750 ml	24 fl oz (1 $^1/_5$ pints)	3 cups
1 litre	32 fl oz (1 $^3/_5$ pints)	4 cups
1.25 litres	40 fl oz (2 pints)	5 cups
1.5 litres	48 fl oz (2 $^2/_5$ pints)	6 cups
2.5 litres	80 fl oz (4 pints)	10 cups

LENGTH

Metric	Imperial
0.5 cm	$^1/_4$ inch
1 cm	$^1/_2$ inch
1.5 cm	$^3/_4$ inch
2.5 cm	1 inch

DRY MEASURES

Metric	Imperial
30 grams	1 ounce
45 grams	1$^1/_2$ ounces
55 grams	2 ounces
70 grams	2$^1/_2$ ounces
85 grams	3 ounces
100 grams	3$^1/_2$ ounces
110 grams	4 ounces
125 grams	4$^1/_2$ ounces
140 grams	5 ounces
280 grams	10 ounces
450 grams	16 ounces (1 pound)
500 grams	1 pound, 1$^1/_2$ ounces
700 grams	1$^1/_2$ pounds
800 grams	1$^3/_4$ pounds
1 kilogram	2 pounds, 3 ounces
1.5 kilograms	3 pounds, 4$^1/_2$ ounces
2 kilograms	4 pounds, 6 ounces

The Publisher wishes to thank Lim's Arts and Living for the loan of their crockery and tableware.

Photographer: Yu Hui Ying

First published as Cook Malaysian, 1980
This edition 2014

Other Marshall Cavendish Offices:
Marshall Cavendish Corporation. 99 White Plains Road, Tarrytown NY 10591-9001, USA • Marshall Cavendish International (Thailand) Co Ltd. 253 Asoke, 12th Flr, Sukhumvit 21 Road, Klongtoey Nua, Wattana, Bangkok 10110, Thailand • Marshall Cavendish (Malaysia) Sdn Bhd, Times Subang, Lot 46, Subang Hi-Tech Industrial Park, Batu Tiga, 40000 Shah Alam, Selangor Darul Ehsan, Malaysia

Marshall Cavendish is a trademark of Times Publishing Limited

National Library Board Singapore Cataloguing in Publication Data

Lee, Sook Ching, author.
Malaysian home cooking : a treasury of authentic Malaysian recipes / Lee Sook Ching.
– Singapore : Marshall Cavendish Cuisine, [2014]
pages cm
First published as Cook Malaysian, 1980.
ISBN : 978-981-4484-22-0 (paperback)

1. Cooking, Malaysian. I. Title.

TX724.5.M4
641.59595 -- dc23   OCN868194616

Printed in Singapore by Craft Print International Ltd